AF266377

Cover photo and Kathryn Girard photos
by Susan Vogelfang

Page design by Anna Myers Sabatini

Paperback ISBN: 978-1-971030-00-5
Ebook ISBN: 978-1-971030-01-2

Green Fire Press
PO Box 377 Housatonic MA 01236

Publisher's Cataloging-in-Publication Data

Names: Girard, Kathryn, author.
Title: It Is Time: The Evolution of Earth and Humanity: Channeled Teachings / Kathryn Girard.
Description: Includes bibliographical references. | Housatonic, MA: Green Fire Press, 2026.
Identifiers: LCCN: 2025927520 | ISBN: 978-1-971030-00-5 (paperback) | 978-1-971030-01-2 (ebook)
Subjects: LCSH Prophecies (Occultism) | Guides (Spiritualism) | Self-help. | BISAC BODY, MIND & SPIRIT / Channeling & Mediumship | BODY, MIND & SPIRIT / Angels & Spirit Guides | BODY, MIND & SPIRIT / Inspiration & Personal Growth | BODY, MIND & SPIRIT / Prophecy | BODY, MIND & SPIRIT / Spiritualism
Classification: LCC BF1809 .G57 2026 | DDC 133.3—dc23

Praise for *IT IS TIME*

In a sweeping call to stretch our hearts, minds, and our fundamental consciousness, *It Is Time* conveys the Teachings of spiritual and extraterrestrial Beings who offer healing for every dimension of human and planetary life. Through Kathryn Girard's skilled channeling, the Teachers map out our planetary situation, including the radical encouragement and instruction we are constantly receiving from the "Other Realm." Girard translates complex Teachings into easily accessible language for her readers still planted on this good Earth. Read this book with a curious and open mind and heart, and it will change you and your life.

> **—Penny Gill**, Professor emerita and former Dean of the College, Mount Holyoke College, and author of *What In the World Is Going On?* and *Radiant Heart of the Cosmos*.

It is Time is the blueprint for the survival and evolution of our planet and mankind. Heed the loving words of these Teachers as they provide instructions and guidance to assist us during this transition. Learn how sending our love and gratitude helps heal our Mother Earth. The Earth and humanity need our hope for the future, our hearts open to love and compassion for all. Now is the time for each of us to be dedicated participants committed to the ascension of the Earth and humanity. Let the Guides show us the way!

> **—Karen Ferris**, Reiki Master teacher, channel and co-owner of True North Wellness, Essex, MA.

In *It Is Time: The Evolution of Earth and Humanity*, channel and teacher Kathryn Girard opens a sacred dialogue between humanity and the higher realms. The book's transmissions—offered by Makel, the Peacekeepers, Andraus & the Light Collective, and the ever-compassionate Kuan Yin—form a symphony of guidance for this pivotal moment in planetary ascension. This book belongs alongside the works of Kryon, the Seth Material, and Conversations with God. It is both timeless and timely: a spiritual map for the heart-centered evolution now unfolding. This is not merely a book to read, but a spiritual companion to live with, opening hearts to co-create the next phase of humanity's story.

—**Elizabeth Foley, Ph.D.**, channel & author of *Awakening the Lightworker Within.* elizabethfoley.com

IT IS TIME

The
Evolution
of Earth
and
Humanity

CHANNELED TEACHINGS

Kathryn Girard

Green
Fire
Press

Housatonic
Massachusetts

CONTENTS

PART THREE: TEACHINGS FROM THE PEACEKEEPERS

PART FOUR: TEACHINGS FROM ANDRAUS AND THE LIGHT COLLECTIVE

FOREWORD

By Diana Muenz Chen

"Trust in Allah and tie your camel." This hadith by Prophet Muhammad reminds us to be open to what the Divine is teaching us, to surrender to Divine wisdom and at the same time to take responsibility for our actions and inner life. We are co-creators with the Divine.

As co-creators, we must do our part, put in the work, and use the resources and abilities our soul has brought into this life. With all the changes happening on the planet and within ourselves, we are faced with strong energy and, profound decisions. We are in this flow of co-creatorship and we need to understand how we can contribute to the unfoldment of the profound shift in which we're taking part.

How do we navigate this teeming energy?

As the founder, with Archangel Michael, of the Open Heart Channeling School in 1988, I have for many years known these two gifted channelers, Kathryn and Laura, along with their high-level spirit guides. I can assure you that you are in good hands. Laura and Kathryn both have the upmost integrity and have strong relationships with their spirit guides, who have urged them to get this book's wisdom out into the world.

In this insightful book, the spirit guides give us detailed information about the deep transformation happening for the Earth and her inhabitants. They deliver an engaging overview and make thoughtful suggestions on how to navigate this shift. Kathryn and Laura, with spirit guides, seamlessly collaborate to bring a shared vision that is presented from the varying angles each contributes.

Besides knowing the channelers, I've come to know and respect their spirit guides, as I've listened to their guides share their wisdom many times. During the years of our work together in the school, their guides have spoken often about important spiritual issues. I have been privileged to learn a great deal from their guidance.

Makel, The Peacekeepers, Andraus and Kuan Yin are extremely dedicated mentors and wise beings, who represent some of the large number of spirit guides who are assisting us at this time. They consider this an urgent time to bring about change and to help us strengthen our ability to create in loving positive ways. They have been intent on helping us as we have been challenged by all the changes within and around us.

These spirit guides speak of how to maintain our positivity, how rightfully to view life on Earth and how to live from love—all very valuable ways of being. They offer exercises and meditations to help with all the myriad changes challenging us now.

These high-level guides touch all the beautiful, sometimes painful parts of creation and our humanity. They share their wisdom to inform us on all levels, including our souls, about the inevitable shift happening on the planet. They give clever and useful metaphors to explain aspects of what they are teaching, such as talking about the experience of being on earth like we are away at school, or that at this time of ascension we are like the olden day pioneers, forging new untrodden pathways, and they add the clever idea to "mind the gap" of stepping into the unknown.

If you open to feel the intention behind the words in this book, you'll have a sense of the importance both channelers and spirit guides place on these messages. We can't ignore these high-level, wise spirit guides, who are urgently calling us into action—to be the co-creators that we are.

It is time!

—**Diana Muenz Chen** is the founder of the Open Heart Channeling School in New York, a highly respected channel and teacher, and the author of *Channeling—The Heart & the Art*, and *Know Your Soul: Bring Joy to Your Life*, with David A. Schwerin. Find out more at Dianamuenzchen.com.

PART ONE

INTRODUCTIONS

HOW THIS BOOK CAME TO BE

Kathryn's story

Though channeling has never been my profession, it has been a deeply enriching aspect of my life and spiritual development. I began my conscious spiritual journey in the mid 1970s, when a friend made an appointment for me to meet with the silent monk, Baba Hari Das. He had a chalk board. I have no idea if I spoke or if he wrote anything. It was as if my heart cracked open and I sobbed until it was time to leave.

That experience began a passionate exploration of spiritual meditation practices, attending workshops and retreats with Buddhist, Hindu, Sufi, and Native American medicine men and women teachers. I was the guest of a Druid high priestess at sacred rituals and gatherings. While I was never attracted to the dogma, rules or forms of particular beliefs or practices, I embraced the sense of expansion and connection to something beyond the material, visible world. Accompanying a friend to a channeling workshop with Roslyn Bruyere in 1986 led to my unexpected awakening as a channel for spirit guides. I began serious training in her program and have been a channel since then.

The nature of my work in the world led me to keep channeling quite separate. While my spirit guide and teacher Kuan Yin and I taught workshops, led small groups and did occasional private sessions, my channeling focused primarily on my own personal and spiritual growth until I retired.

Spirit guides have different purposes. Amun was the first spirit being I met. He is my gatekeeper, my protector and guardian. When I was developing my ability to channel, I had a guide I called Amaxus who explained he worked with new channels to smooth the way. There was 'The Healer' who brought forward extremely powerful transformative energies, but as I opened my abilities to receive their energies more fully, our energies were not fully aligned and we had to part.

Decades ago, I had a guide who wanted to bring forward material about climate and earth changes. I wasn't ready and declined. Then there have been guides with whom I have had a deeper relationship and an openness to their purposes in being with me. During an emotionally difficult time, Thelson arrived to provide weekly sessions focused on releasing fears and old emotional issues. Amatawa came to be with me to push me into stepping forward and owning what I could contribute. She definitely helped me, but my resistance definitely frustrated her. The Ansari came in 2020 to let me know it was time to step off the cliff and fly with greater freedom. As gentle as they were, their message scared me. But I was ready. They let me know when their work with me was done and they moved on.

I am constantly working to refine my channeling, and as I do so I am joined by new teachers whose purposes can be served in our work together. Currently I actively work with a team of teachers. Kuan Yin, who anchors my compassion and heart, and Makel, my very patient and wise healer, are long-time companions. Melchizedek, present over the last four years, guides not only what I teach but what I learn from teaching. Archangel Michael has not only guided my work with clients, but also my connection with my soul and the Divine. Archangel Metatron has helped to extend the vibrations I can open to.

The Idea of the Book

That's how we get to this book, which was quite honestly not my idea. Makel indicated that they wanted to do a book on the evolution of the Earth and humanity, because of the energies gathering to support movement to a higher dimensional[1] plane. In watching my reaction to addressing evolutionary changes, Makel understood that focusing on healing and starting with the Earth would be an easier way in for me and many others. Below is Makel's message to me from November 2020, about how a book would move forward.

> So you wish to address the subject of the book. Well, your interest in writing has offered us an opportunity, as we are interested in the possibility of teaching and providing additional direction or support to those who are open to the idea of healing the Earth as part of the transition underway. Although this is not what you would call your expertise, and we know it makes you nervous, it is indeed our expertise and we would be happy to bring forward more information, suggestions, and possibilities for people who are concerned about the healing of the planet.
>
> And yes, there is the possibility for others to participate in any such effort, and we think this is a very exciting opportunity. It is as if you will be the panel moderator. We will have a conversation with other Teachers about how best to proceed, because we see that you are willing to proceed and this is an excellent format for going forward.

---

1 A higher dimensional plane than Earth would be a less dense state of existence operating at and supporting a higher frequency and vibrational state

The Peacekeepers and Andraus Step Forward

The Peacekeepers, a group new to me, responded to Makel's invitation. They are a group of extraterrestrial beings from many different systems. They share a common purpose of assisting the Earth and humanity during this important time of transition.

Andraus and the Light Collective, a collective of high vibration healers and teachers focused on humanity's evolution, also came forward with a practice for individuals and groups aligned with the vibrational changes underway. Andraus is channeled by Laura Craig, a colleague of mine.

Laura is a channel, healer and lawyer whose story of channeling started when she moved to New York City for work in 1993, and through friends met Diana Muenz Chen, a channel and healer. Laura has studied channeling with Diana and the Open Heart Channeling School since 1995 and has her own healing practice. In talking about what channeling means to her and why she feels compelled to bring Andraus' work forward now, Laura said:

"My experience is that there is much more to this world than simply our finite, physical and intellectual selves. Our experience of prayer and meditation brings us closer to the Divine through our spiritual selves. In sharing my journey with Andraus, I would like to offer a pathway that can bring a sense of balance, peace and centeredness in daily life. Andraus' pathway brings clarity, wisdom, space, energy, love, peace, joy and a sense of renewal. In recent years our focus on intellectual and scientific viewpoints has detached us from the larger collective reality. I would like to share my experience and what Andraus has channeled through me as a real and valuable process that can bring a sense of centeredness, connection, energy and joy to all our lives. In these channelings, Andraus and the Light Collective teach us all a daily practice to provide a pathway through these turbulent and transitional times."

It became clear very quickly that Laura and I were brought together so that the teachings of Andraus and the Light Collective could be disseminated through Makel's book initiative.

The Nature of the Book

From there it all unfolded and here we are, with a book about the transition that the Earth and humanity are currently experiencing from three different perspectives holding a common purpose. In spiritual terms the book is about the ascension[2] of the Earth and humanity to a higher dimensional plane. The guides provide suggestions on how we can contribute to helping the Earth and humanity to reach a higher level of functioning. Because so much depends on us, their teachings address how we, as human beings who yearn for more connection, kindness and love as the guiding energies of human interaction, can continue to grow, develop and find peace in an environment of dramatic changes and rising fears.

---

2   In spiritual terms, Ascension with a capital A refers to the movement and expansion of a soul into connection with the All That Is. Ascended Masters are beings who have progressed to this ability but choose to hold a focus of expression for purposes of continuing to guide other souls or serve creation purposes in other ways. There is an ongoing process of ascending (small a) in vibration and capacity along this path.

The book consists of transcripts of messages channeled from 2020 to the present. Laura and I both had obstacles to overcome as our teachers' messengers. Challenges arose due to some discomfort with both the subject of the book, which felt overwhelming, and with the addition of the energies of The Peacekeepers for me, and the Light Collective for Laura. As channels, we are the translators for the higher vibration spirit beings with whom we communicate. And in the end, as always, we simply had to surrender and trust.

Personal Impact on Kathryn and Laura

Channeling our teachers on this subject has changed Laura and me. I find myself feeling and expressing a deeper level of gratitude to the Earth. I now have a broader perspective in which to view all the sadness, greed, fear, anger, hatred and climate disruption that fills the news and rises in response to it. It is not easy to hold love and compassion forward, but seeing all the upheaval as a reaction to and stage of the transformation underway for both the Earth and humanity has helped me. I understand what I can contribute. I see Laura and myself as two very, very small parts of a very, very large gathering of midwives who will, along with you and all who hold an awareness of the light within, enable this birthing into a new platform from which humans can grow, create, connect.

Laura has been working regularly with the exercises and following the steps for soul connection set out by Andraus. She says: "I have been journaling about my experience of following the practices of soul connection that Andraus lays out. It is slightly different on each occasion. Sometimes it takes time to let go of my to-do list for the day but it is lovely to focus on grounding. I feel so much more energy in my feet, my belly and through my body, and it brings an upsurge of energy, heat and connection.

"Bringing this energy through my body is nourishing and energizing. I intend to connect to spirit and I feel that connection in my heart. It is a lovely, warm, peaceful experience—supportive, encouraging, calming, and centering. There is more clarity and confidence.

"I hope you will give this a try and use this practice regularly with other exercises in this book, all of which invite you to participate in this great transition in ways that are easily incorporated into your regular daily life."

THE GUIDES INTRODUCE THEMSELVES

Makel

We will begin. We have had many names of course, over what you would consider time, but which we consider experience. Our experiences are now assembled and integrated, but they were acquired from a variety of perspectives and those perspectives had different names, none of which matter to us at this point. You know, on our plane of existing one does not need to introduce oneself. One simply is. When one encounters other energies, they are simply understood. Yes, it is very different. We do not need to extend a hand, say our name and then describe our job or position. So how shall your readers encounter us? How shall we speak what is important for them to understand?

We are a being on a plane of existence where we can offer and make available a variety of support. Our support takes the form of assistance primarily with healing energies. But these healing energies are not what you on the earth plane think of as healing. You think of cures. You think of something that is taken in or done that then effects a result that you call healing. And it is true that the medicines that you take allow the resolution of certain specific physiological problems. While our energies can concern themselves with those physiological issues and problems, our focus is on the greater whole in which all is connected.

We seek to intervene in the interconnected energetic patterns, and we focus on the disruption of the healthy expression of the pattern as a whole. We bring our energies forward to assist in the understanding of the whole, to assist in the healing that is not amenable to the Western medicines or even to the other forms of medicines arising from the Far East. None are able to be fully holistic in addressing the many layers of the pattern through which disruption is expressed. What you think of as a disease or a physiological problem or even a mental or emotional problem does not exist on only one level. It exists all the way through the entire being on all energetic and physiological levels, including patterns predating the current life.

So we are Makel and we are present on our plane of being to bring to the Earth plane greater understanding of the larger patterns and layers of the whole system. Even when we are dealing with an individual with a particular problem, we are bringing energies to the whole system, looking at the disruption of the pattern in its many layers. So, yes, we are primarily focused on healing. But healing within the energetic holism of the being and the planet.

When we were coming forward to work with this one, Kathryn, many, many years ago, we came forth solely as a guide to assist her with her initial work of distance healing. She discontinued that particular work for a time. Nevertheless, we stayed present for her as one of the guides that she would see in her sanctuary and she identified us as an assistant for healing. Over time, other guides came forward and we receded. We had other work to do. However, we maintained our connection.

More recently we came forward again, initially to assist with her own healing. And then we were able to introduce ourselves as a teacher for more than just personal physiological healing and were able to communicate our interest in planetary healing and our interest in providing support and guidance to others who are aware of the importance of the Earth's healing at this moment.

There are many energies assembled in support of the Earth, both energies on the planet and those of beings not embodied on the planet. Our work has always had the thread of healing and our work has always been focused primarily on the Earth plane. We are currently part of an impetus for healing that is bringing to the Earth support, encouragement and guidance for the Earth's healing and the evolution of the Earth and humanity.

We have had lives embodied, embodied on the Earth plane. We have worked as a healer on the Earth plane at a time when there were many energies to draw from. We were able to be present when the creation energies of the Earth were very dynamic and the human structure able to hold a soul's energy emerged. As you can imagine, when you are wanting to work with healing energies, the palpable creation energies are very powerful tools. Instead of the medicines that you now depend upon, there was energy available that could be used. Much of what was needed was the presence of energies that would open and calm, so that being in such a dense body was not frightening. This was needed when embodiment on the Earth was relatively new. We are not talking about what you call cavemen, although that was a certainly a difficult transition time, but in the very earliest of civilizations that were being peopled by souls who had no experience with a third dimensional existence. Being in a physical body on the Earth was very different than embodiment in other places.

Earth was created for separation, for division, for dichotomies and dualities and so when souls were embodied onto the Earth plane, it was very frightening. It evoked fears—many, many fears. Healing during that transformative time used the creation energies that were very, very active and present, channeling them into the energetic fields of those who were ready to be benefited. It was a very specific process and those receiving healing were very specifically selected, and that was, you could say, our job. Our job was to go among and identify those in need, and then to channel the energies that would calm the being, calm the spirit, feed the spirit so that the being could go forth to accomplish what was identified as their purpose.

This is a different time, but one that has been long anticipated. It is a time of utmost importance and our purpose remains much the same in the service of the evolution of humanity and the Earth.

The Peacekeepers

This is an interesting experiment. You want us to introduce ourselves for the purposes of your book. We understand that this will be important no matter how our messages are shared, because people will want to know if they can trust the message. You are the messenger, but we are also the messenger. So we all must provide information that will assist those who are perhaps ready to receive.

We are not like Makel. We are not a single being who has lived on the Earth and is now working in spirit, reaching back down to those who are embodied. We are a group. We are not of the Earth. We come from other systems, other planes of existence, larger energy systems outside of the Earth. And we, along with many others from many systems outside the Earth, have watched the Earth's energies with compassion, concern and the desire to assist. We wish to assist the Earth and those who are upon the Earth because it is in the interest of the larger whole, the whole that is not understood by those who are within the Earth template.

Our purposes do have to do with the greater healing of the Earth, but in connection with the energies that the Earth is connected to. The Earth influences and is being influenced by larger energies. In addition to that, planet Earth is affected by all that comes from the Earth, flows into the Earth, surrounds the Earth, all of the feelings, all of the experiences of all that is on the Earth. So, it has many layers.

But when you are thinking down into the Earth, you are thinking about concrete structures. We are not thinking about concrete structures. We are thinking about energetic structures that are both of the Earth, but also not of the Earth. We are not exactly a buffer between the Earth and other planets, galaxies, other objects and existences in the outer world, but in a sense, we are a bridge of energies because we have what we would call a proper need to align the energies with healing. It benefits not only the Earth and all on the Earth, but also the greater system of all creation.

All of spirit, all beings are concerned, not just those closely connected with the current Earth planetary alignments. Concerned and invested. Invested? Yes, that is the word. Invested in an outcome that is beneficial for all. There are pathways open for greater benefit and pathways that will be more constrained and problematic. So we are here to encourage and support the openings in more and more of those who are currently on the Earth plane. We are working with all of the beings surrounding the Earth and, yes, we are not just focused on Earth. Our concerns are more broad, far-reaching. But for now, the focus is on Earth. The focus is on what is happening in the constellation of frequency alignments.

We are not one being, but many, many beings. We have assembled because when we all connect our energy is much stronger. Since we communicate primarily through vibrations and frequencies, the process of turning this into your words is not simple. By coming together and amassing our energies and our experiences of energetic transmission and frequency attunement we are able to funnel our ideas and our guidance more easily. In this way it is easier for us to draw the attention of those who would be capable of receiving our messages and communicating them on the Earth plane. In truth, when you are reading these words they are infused with a vibration. And it is that vibration that is carrying the weight, the force and the impact of the words. Words are simply vehicles for carrying energy and our work is to shift energy. So when you are reading these words, you are, to varying degrees, receiving the frequency and vibration that is important for what is to come.

Our existences have been in many different places, in many different forms, but always where the primary consciousness was that of vibration and frequency. None of the origins of our various species were similar to the density of energy and form from which humanity and the Earth are evolving. We are here because of our collective evolutionary experience, and because what is needed now is a change in vibration and frequency for the Earth. Our interest is in assisting the Earth to be part of a higher frequency that will be of greater benefit, not just to those who are now or will be upon the planet, but of benefit to all the others who exist outside of the Earth plane. Our energies are what you would call benevolent. Our messages carry a certain urgency because we are seeing the larger effects of the current state of the Earth. We seek to facilitate and support the direction of the Earth's ascension to higher frequencies that will lead to differences in the embodiments of those who will continue to come to the Earth for their learning. Our messages are here to encourage and support the energies necessary to bring about this important and significant transformation.

What we will be sharing relates to changing vibrations and frequencies, and this is something that all of you can both receive and contribute to. If you are reading these words, then already your energy is gathering and beginning its own shift. Because while you think that things take a great deal of time they do not. And you can be energetically receptive whether or not your mind is receptive.

We do not have an English name. Nor do we have a name in any of the other languages. Who we are is a vibration that is created by the energies of all those who are assembled in our collective intention and agreement. So. If you were to try to perceive us you would simply see patterns of vibration. You may call us The Peacekeepers.

Andraus

I am Andraus. I am a member of The Light Collective, and I come as a guide. My background comes from lifetimes on this Earth. I have been a guide for Laura many, many times. We know each other well. I am also part of a larger healing collective that wishes to bring forward this work to guide everyone with an interest in finding a pathway forward at this transitional time. Laura is able to channel my energies, as well as the larger energies of the Light Collective within which I am working.

As The Light Collective, we are here to assist with the evolutionary work that it is happening and to give teachings about how best to move forward in the current climate. We have no connection to race or gender. We have no political aims and no vibration of difference or division. We are a collective of light beings who come together to promote healing within the human sphere.

We are a large group with great wisdom and light who bring structure around concepts that might seem difficult and perhaps a little abstract. This structure enables us to bring this wisdom into the human realm with clarity.

My channelings can be clear and concise because I am part of this larger whole that holds the structure so that it can be brought forward in ways that make sense. It is exciting to be part of this group because it brings a great clarity of vision, concept and message.

Kuan Yin

We choose to introduce ourselves by our essence, the central energies or vibrations evoked by the name Kuan Yin. We are a being of compassion, of unconditional love. We hear with compassion and we hold in an embrace of love the pain and suffering of those on the Earth plane. But we also hear the yearning for connection, for an open heart that is larger than what is often referred to as the emotions of the heart.

Our service to humanity stretches back many millennia, but the changes that are currently unfolding will allow the flowering of greater love, greater compassion, gentleness and a sense of connection to all. Much of what the soul knows is lost when you are born into the density of the Earth. This allowed for a great deal of learning and growth born of experiencing and releasing pain and suffering. A new time arises. The Earth can become a planet where love grows and fear recedes. We are present to speak to how to open your heart to the guidance in this book, to ever-greater light and to your contribution to this potential future.

HOW TO READ AND BENEFIT FROM THIS BOOK

Kathryn's suggestions for reading the teachings from Makel and The Peacemakers

The teachers' messages are unified about the nature of the transition we are in the midst of but their emphases and 'voices' are each unique in themselves. Find the teacher that resonates with you.

Makel and The Peacemakers brought teachings forward in their own timing and sequence. Their teachings can be read in the order presented, but you can also scan the detailed list of teachings in the Contents and find a message that calls to you. Go to that message and if there is an idea or a phrase that stops you, stay with that and don't worry about finishing the page.

You can also simply place your intention and desire on finding what in the messages will benefit you. Then open to a seemingly random page.

The teachers communicate through energy. The words are doorways into the energy that is the heart of the teachers' communications. The messages of the teachers are best encountered with an expectation of allowing the words, their meaning and their energy to be heard and understood by your heart, not your head.

I wouldn't recommend reading more than two at a time. Simple practices are suggested by Makel and The Peacemakers. Try them and see what fits.

Laura's suggestions for reading the Andraus teachings

The Andraus messages are different, in that this section of the book intends to teach you a daily practice to connect with your soul and to give you a pathway to remain centered in challenging times. You are encouraged to read right through the Andraus materials to gain an overview of where you are being led forward, and then check in with yourself: are you moved to try these exercises?

Kuan Yin's guidance on opening to the teachings

Kuan Yin offers some guidance before you begin and an Afterword as a reminder of the importance of approaching this work and absorbing the teachings through your heart. Kuan Yin's messages can be reread any time you want support for settling, opening, calming your own energies or for absorbing what you have experienced.

BEFORE YOU BEGIN:
KUAN YIN'S MESSAGE TO YOU

We are Kuan Yin and we are pleased to have been invited to speak to you directly as you begin to encounter what is offered through the words in this book. It is our purpose in speaking with you to give you a sense of what is asked of you. Many books are important because of the ideas they bring to your mind and the new knowledge that can attach to existing structures of knowledge in your mind. This book is different in that it will ask you to let go of what you think you know, to let go of the structures that derive from the forms that are part of this world in which you live.

This book brings forth different ways of understanding what is happening in your world right now. It asks you to not respond out of fear, to not get caught up in the idea of what is being lost. Instead, it asks you to open to an unseen, as-yet-unknown-to-you potential. We understand this is difficult for the mind. It is not difficult for the heart.

We do not speak of the organ in your body, nor the heart that you see as a place holding wounds, and desires, and vulnerabilities. No, we speak of the heart that holds love not just for the self, but for the larger world. The part of you that holds to a hope for peace, for kindness, for gentleness, that can hear these words not just as concepts or disappointments or frustrations, but rather as their essence: the essence of kindness, the essence of gentleness, the essence of love.

We ask that as you begin this book, you choose to soften your existing ideas. Soften your expectations and open your heart to hope, to potentials not yet known but so needed.

You are living in a very difficult, complicated world where much is being lost, much is being destroyed, and the beauty of the world and of human beings is being supplanted by corruption, destruction, greed, disconnection, separation. Amid all the disturbing news of the day, this book offers a way of understanding. It shares a larger view of creation energies in their ongoing trajectory of evolving, bringing the evolution of the Earth and humanity to a new foundation for human experience that supports more gentleness, more kindness, more love.

We ask that you, as a reader, shift from your normal perspective of seeking to test new ideas against what you know. We ask you to open your heart and let your heart find its pathway to hope for a new and better future for the Earth and humanity.

You will have much unseen support for you as you embark on this adventure. We know how difficult a time this is, and how much is being asked of you now. Know that it is being asked of you because you hold that seed of hope, that seed of potential. This book contains energies to support the growth of hope and potential in you.

TEACHINGS FROM MAKEL

MOVING TO A NEW DIMENSION

When we look at who this book is for, we see the light in those who do not yet know how to connect, expand and contribute.[3] We are reaching out to those whose light is ready to burn brighter, at a higher volume and with a greater contribution.

This book goes out to those of you who know you have a purpose—who know that you are on Earth to be of help—but how to do this remains still hidden from you. Our purpose in this book is to give you some direction in uncovering and knowing your purpose and how to meet it as the Earth is changing.

This requires you to open not your mind but your heart—to read, interpret and understand these words through your heart. The words are simply ways of providing you with energies to which your being can respond. There are many ways to express kindness and compassion in your world, and we encourage you to be as kind and compassionate in your everyday life as you are able to be, but we also ask that you seek to express kindness and compassion no matter what is occurring in the world. We see the greater stage of the Earth, the greater human stage, as your stage for expression and response.

---

3   Light refers to the essence of the Divine, of Divine Love that is part of the soul essence within all human beings. Those who function with awareness of this are often called lightworkers

The Earth and humanity have reached a tipping point in energies. It will feel to most people that the dark forces of greed, corruption, rage and war are winning, overtaking and destroying all that has been good. We are one of many voices here to tell you that what you see in the escalation of what feels dark and dangerous is in fact a sign of change for the better.

We do not want to scare you. Quite the opposite: we wish to grant you the information and knowing that will resonate with what a part of you already knows. The Earth is shifting from its current orientation as a third-dimensional place to a higher dimension.[4] The centerpiece of the new dimensional reality for humans will be increased support for connection, spiritual understanding, love, compassion and kindness as what is valued and rewarded in your communities. You cannot be expected to know this, but we will, in these pages, guide you to greater understanding.

We are joined by many on the Earth and in spirit form in the enterprise of supporting the coming changes. There have been times when we all told our own truths and focused on teaching humans at their next level of readiness. Our messages were on different subjects, different foci. This is a unique time in that we all—spirit guides, ascended masters, archangels, extraplanetary beings from across the galaxies—are present with the same message: *It is time.*

The human species is preparing to advance to a new dimension. The Earth is preparing to move to a new dimension. Every birth needs midwives. These evolutionary movements of the Earth and humanity require many midwives to ensure the delivery. There are those that are against this change, for they have much to lose. The rules for

---

4   A 3rd dimensional plane refers to a state of existence characterized by lower frequencies, density of forms, dualities, and less awareness of higher vibrations and energies.

winning, as they would see it, will be disrupted if hate, war, greed, fear and separation are no longer supported. If love, kindness and compassion gain ascendency, if the awareness of oneness becomes the new heartbeat, what happens to the old rules?

You already use this term disruption to mean a new way of doing business. Exactly so. The business of being a human and the business of being on the planet are being disrupted by new energies flooding in. Your light, the light that this book will encourage you to brighten and let shine, is part of that disruptive energy. You are here to shine the way for the Earth and humanity to ascend.

There is nothing for you to fear

The question before us is how to communicate what will be occurring during the ascension to a new dimension without evoking fear.

Dear ones, there is nothing to fear if you believe that you are in your essence the manifestation of your soul, that all that occurs is what has always been the potential for you in this lifetime. There have always been possibilities and potentials for your being. As you have learned and acquired experiences and learned more, the possibilities and potentials for your lifetime have altered, adjusted, opened or closed. But always new possibilities and potentials open out of what you have experienced and, more importantly, learned.

Some experiences are weighted, you might say, with stronger energies but your decisions at any point can shift the energy flowing into different potentials. Clearly, what surrounds you affects your possibilities. Some of what surrounds you reflects your own life choices and patterns, but you also exist in the field of much larger patterns. The ascension of the Earth and humanity is one such larger pattern in which you exist.

As with your own life, the possibilities and potential of the ascension moving forward has been affected by humans. You are a part of the human will, intention and expression that opens, closes, pushes or retards the progress toward the ascension. In reading this now you are choosing to fulfill your role or to take another step in fulfilling your role in moving the ascension forward. That you have light to bring to the ascension energies does not mean that you will not potentially suffer the effects of the resistance to the changing energies of the planet. Know that where you are and what you encounter and what you bring to those experiences is all part of your soul's purposes. You are here on this planet now to participate.

There are those who are here participating in the resistance to the changes ascension will bring to humanity because they are filled with fear. Those who live with greed, anger, rage, hate, and a closed heart live with fear. To them, love, compassion, kindness, generosity and open-hearted connection to others means loss of self, loss of status, loss of dominance. Indeed, those losses will occur insofar as their understanding comes from a limited perspective on where true power resides and what success in life means.

Many will leave their embodiments, for their souls and their higher selves have reached an accord that further participation will not be valuable, that the lessons and experiences intended have been reached or cannot be reached. There will be many opportunities for exiting. This is necessary. You cannot have what is new emerge without what was present being overwritten, replaced, destroyed.

Destruction is such a terrible word within your world for often there is no positive creation emerging from what humans destroy. In the plan of the ascension, the positive creation energies are vibrant, glowing with the higher vibrations of unconditional love and connectedness of all that is. What is gone is replaced by the new vibrant energy. You are already a part of that new vibrant energy that is coming forth in this early phase of transition to a new higher dimension for the Earth and humanity.

Our purpose here is to provide you with both information and ideas that will enable you to choose to keep open your connection to the ascension energies and even strengthen your expression and connection to them.

You have an unlimited potential to open to these new energies. We would say that is why you are interested in these words. A part of you yearns to move forward into these energies more fully and to experience the grace and the joy of being a pioneer in this important change for the Earth and humanity. As we go forward, we will provide you with ways you can do this for your own being, for humanity overall and for the Earth. Welcome to the new human, of whom you are an early representative.

If you are 'the new human,' then what does that mean you are supposed to be thinking, feeling, doing? We want to help you focus on the parts of you that represent this new human, to help you build the muscles of the new human and to guide you to the joy of this way of being. As you do this for yourself you will be assisting the Earth and all of humanity. We will also offer suggestions on how you may more directly serve the Earth's transitions as well as the larger human movement of change.

Is this too much? It is not too much for you and that is why you are here and why you are reading this book. Your soul intended to participate in this. It is one of the larger purposes that you hold as a mission in this lifetime. You have many purposes, but this is one that is shared by vast numbers of those on this planet, those who are coming on to this planet and have been for the past three decades. You are not alone.

Conscience and consciousness

We ask you to consider what it means to be two things: 1) a being with consciousness; and 2) a being with conscience. When we are talking about consciousness, we are talking about that human ability to be aware, consider, think through, feel, and choose. There is a certain responsibility that consciousness brings with it, especially in the current time, which is a time of evolutionary change.

Evolution has been ongoing. As it is understood by your sciences, it occurs by genetic mutations and variations, changing environments that then trigger new strengths while old strengths fade in importance. You see this easily in the animal and other kingdoms where new patterns of coloring or behaviors arise because they are more successful in some way. They endure and multiply and become the new standard.

When we come to consciousness, there is more awareness in making choices about what is valued, what is put forward as desirable, what is nurtured in its expression, what is to be prized. Over time, then, what is consciously chosen becomes the template—the genetic template and the energy template.

You can see how a template for human beings has developed. Looking at those who are most successful, it would seem that template of individual striving and the values that support individualism, have all been reinforced. Aspects having to do with greed and the attributes that support acquiring more power, more material possessions, more wealth have made an imprint across different cultures in different parts of the world, though there are culturally influenced variations on the template. But those whose energy template is very different—for example, think of the indigenous peoples—those templates are not valued, by and large.

So there has been a choice and an allowing, and now you are living with the outcome of those choices and the templates that have been supported for human behavior. But we come now to a moment where that template for human behavior—power over another, achievement over another at their expense, the caring for the self no matter the cost, human, planetary, or other life forms—no longer serves the greater good. Because there are enough of you who want a different template for humanity, the evolutionary change for humanity and the planet has already begun.

You have consciousness, which is why you are able to both experience and choose a different way of being and a different vibrational awareness. And you also have conscience. That is, you have that internal compass of what is right. It starts with what is right for the self. But when you have the consciousness of the greater good, your compass of rightness—your conscience—adjusts to consider more outside the self. This has always been a part of human potential and experience. Empathy, connection with another, moves you to a higher level because it embraces not a one-to-one interaction, but the interaction and knowing of the self as part of a much larger whole. The evolutionary requirement for consciousness and conscience is that movement to fuller, broader, deeper connection, and seeing in that path a future unfolding that is more beneficial for all.

Your responsibility as a person of consciousness and conscience is to keep choosing in your own being connection to a greater whole: caring for and participating in the well-being of all and allowing the compass of what is right to be guided by a sense of a much bigger light.

What you think of as the moral compass is capable of opening to an ever-greater energy of light and knowing within you. You should not allow that to frighten you. It does not mean that you must put yourself in harm's way. It is important for you to know the power of just being. Holding yourself in that awareness, choosing that light as the opening, guiding energy of your being, that is what the energy of this message is about—that sense of Being. When you are in that place, you experience the evolutionary transformation that you are helping to bring forward.

Soften your assumptions

It is difficult to explain what the Earth is to those who are in a solid form and only know the Earth from their in-form perceptions, their physical senses. This does not bring forth the truth of what is being seen. You see what you expect to see. You see with assumptions of what is. You trust your reliance on definitions of what and how things are.

A first step toward seeing more clearly is to loosen your sense of defined boundaries. This is a key on many layers, is it not? It is a key to social relationships, to communities that function smoothly. It is a key to knowing oneself truly—not the idea of oneself as given to you by others or by the stories you tell about yourself. You see the Earth through what you have been told by your physical senses as well as by the experiences of others, by your sciences. All of that serves you for walking on the planet as you have been doing, but it will not serve you as you participate in the evolution and healing of the planet, the evolution of humanity and the evolution of your own essence. What will serve you is choosing to open to new definitions and to soften your assumptions.

The Earth is not as you think of it. You are not the form that others see or that you yourself see in the mirror. You see yourself and define yourself by how others see you—by your job, your home, your family, the words you speak and the words you write. These things define how you see and know yourself and how others see and know you. Yet you know yourself too by what you feel inside. Those feelings do not have a form. They are not concrete. You are also seen and known by others by how you make them feel, by what they experience as your moods and emotions, and these too are not concrete. They do not have a physical form and yet you know them to be real. So you are made up of the concrete, the physical, as well as the unseen, the ephemeral—that which is not seen but moves inside and outside of you.

You may already know yourself to have a soul and an aura of energies. You might know yourself to have a purpose for this life. You may believe in karma and think that you work in this life and will continue to work in other incarnations to learn and to heal past wounds. If so, then you know even more strongly that the unseen energies are greater than what is tangible and that those energies are a part of you as whole.

Likewise, the Earth is a being of form but also of larger unseen energies—not just those unseen mechanisms of magnetic and electric fields. The Earth is an entity with a purpose, driven by creation energies to grow, to manifest, to develop not just in physical expression but in the vibrational quality of existence.

The purpose of this book

We are gathering with others in preparation for the energies that are advancing. We are wanting to make progress, to assist with the healing. Given the current energies, we want to communicate information that would help those who are desperately wanting to have a beneficial impact on the Earth. This is not just because there are individuals for whom this is important. From our perspective, the Earth itself is at a critical junction and what will occur for the Earth is important for all beings. There is a tremendous amount of attention within the higher dimensional planes.

The Earth has been an important venue for developing, and it is beneficial in many ways. Life on the planet has been dependent on the Earth and its resources, as well as life force and healing energies. At present these are increasingly depleted because of the intrusions and misuse and lack of return, we could say, by humans to the Earth. For the future of the Earth and its contributions, we want to assist the Earth's healing. This means, in part, preparing people for what will be a very difficult time.

To heal itself, the Earth must take action. It is not conscious in the sense of 'I will make a hurricane, I will make an earthquake, I'm going to punish the people of Los Angeles for using too much water.' It is not like that. Rather, from the center of the Earth, moving outward, there are energies that cannot find right expression because of what has been done on the Earth. Yet, they must be expressed. And through those expressions there is the possibility of healing because there is the possibility for the Earth to return to a more natural functioning in its movements.

Remember, everything is movement. Air is movement, water is movement, earth is movement, fire is movement.

The Earth needs movement. Natural movements have always happened, and populations of animals, birds, insects and humans have always been affected. But now the impacts are much greater, because of the nature of the impact of humans on the Earth. The number affected is much greater, as is the fear that arises. We wish to provide resources to assist those of you on the Earth to understand the needs of the Earth, the actions of the Earth and the consequences that will arise.

At the same time, we wish to gather those who can focus their energies on the healing of the Earth without needing to focus on how that healing is manifested. We wish to encourage giving back to the Earth without expectation—not in order to prevent earthquakes, hurricanes, tornadoes, fires. It is giving back to the Earth out of gratitude. It is recognizing one's own connection to the Earth, as well as to the heavens and allowing that connection to be strong. When that connection is strong, the Earth is strengthened and benefited, as are you.

What the Earth must do to heal and evolve

Today we take up the topic of the Earth changes that you will be experiencing and those that will be unseen but are of critical importance. Let us begin with what will not be seen by human eyes but will be monitored and observed by those from higher dimensions. There are beings who are concerned and have responsibilities for assisting and intervening where possible on behalf of the Earth's potential development, in alignment with far longer timeframes than you can imagine, since we do not have time as you have structured it.

The Earth is composed of that which can be seen and that which exists but is not seen. You have your sound waves, your frequencies over which different types of communications travel. You are aware of light waves and know that light travels, yet none of these things in their essence can be seen or heard by the human senses. Just so, the Earth is composed not only of matter made visible, but by resonances with vibrations that emanate initially from outside the physical plane and yet penetrate through it. Magnetic resonances—magnetic grids, what is referred to as the crystalline grid—and electrical patterns connect all the parts, down to the subatomic particles that are a part of the Earth's core and all its creations.

You concern yourselves with what you can see and observe, but the Earth's inter-elemental connections are quite complex. Try imagining what it means that the Earth is one being and that every aspect of being is in resonance with every other element, every aspect, every atom. You are one being with every cell in your body holding a connection to the whole of your full being. You think of the cells as separate and yet in truth they are all part of a connected whole. Each cell holds connection to the whole because they are one. This is the hardest concept to explain because in your third-dimensional world you separate everything. You deconstruct an object or a body and then you see all the separateness and fail to go deep enough to understand that each separate part is connected, not just in how its function affects the part next to it, but that each cell is connected to the oneness. We fail in trying to communicate this accurately through your words. You are connected to everything that exists anywhere, anytime—past, present and future. The separations you experience are temporary.

Back to the Earth. The Earth is in motion in the electromagnetic fields that operate within. Just as when you are physically growing, the structures of your body change to allow and create longer bones and larger organs, so the Earth's form is pushing changes from the inside out. At the level you can observe, you see the changes being made in the terrain, in the water shapes and configurations. These are more the result of trying to eliminate that which is damaging or nonbeneficial for the creation energies, or to modify that which is blocking or impeding the Earth's creation energies. The waters, the soil, and the air all need to be cleansed in order to open to greater creation energies.

The Earth will do what it can, but humans will be part of the work on the surface levels. They will be doing this to help the Earth but also to help all of humanity, for without the Earth's abundance of resources how will the population of Earth feed and shelter itself? The past efforts to use the Earth's resources have not been in alignment with service to the greater whole of humanity or the Earth. As the ascension energies increase their presence, humans will begin to address the needs in a less localized and more global way, with a view toward sustaining healthy life for the Earth and for all beings.

This is contrary to the history of the developed nations. It is the old, community Earth-connected way. That way of living has been put down as primitive and impossible to apply to larger scales. Indeed, it is not workable if the goal is the benefit of the few over the many. But that very lower-density way of thinking is what is changing. What is arising is the view that inclusion, the holding of the well-being of all, is the highest goal, the honorable and right way to approach any problem, any opportunity. This is the heart of the future human. This is the human being who will partner with the Earth.

In order to bring this about, the Earth will be withdrawing some of its existing resources, which have already been seriously damaged. Earth forms will collapse, fires will burn to clear and allow new possibilities to emerge. Waters will disappear. There will be Earth-caused crises that are at their root man-made crises. The enormity of these events will evoke, in increasing numbers of hearts, the desire for a different way of going forward. Helping thy neighbor will not just be a saying but a desire alive in many hearts that were previously only inwardly focused. The idea of who is a neighbor will keep extending. There are so many who already feel the pain and suffering of others who are miles and nations away geographically, yet next door in their hearts. Those desires to help will be one important response to the crises that will keep the momentum of the ascension energies growing.

So, you can see that the Earth's body is in the process of changes internally (both the energetic resonances and the physical manifestations of those resonances) and externally on surface. The surface changes stem from the need to address damage that limits what its creations can provide. Just as humanity will live with a new consciousness in the higher dimension, so too will the Earth. But as we have said, this new human and this new Earth can only occur if their energies are joined in the process of change and ascension.

Walking in gratitude

For those who are concerned about the planet, for those who want to improve the health of the planet and all that lives upon the planet, we want to begin with some of the simplest things that one can do physically. Many of you know about walking meditation, where each step is taken with great consciousness and awareness—not thought, but quietness, attending to each foot as it reaches the Earth. For many people, this is not a comfortable practice because the mind wants to be involved in almost everything. That is quite understandable given the way human beings are constructed when they come into form on this planet.

Even for those who do not wish to engage in quiet walking meditation, you can still keep in mind your relation to the Earth while you walk. Gravity holds your feet to the ground, whether that ground is a cement floor or a wooden floor or any kind of floor, no matter how many stories up from the ground. As you walk, have in mind a heartfelt gratitude to the Earth. From your heart to your mind or your mind to your heart, take this idea—because the mind likes to be engaged with ideas—of wanting to plant gratitude.

Every time you take a walk—from your desk to the next room, when you are outside walking your pet, or walking with a friend—have the intention that each time you take a step, you leave an imprint of gratitude. Just hold the intention, when you start walking, to plant gratitude with each step. In this way, you embed gratitude into the soil. Your feet, as they carry you, carry gratitude.

Your intention to plant gratitude can be reinforced each time it flows back into your mind.

'Oh, yes, I am walking with gratitude for the Earth that holds me here, that supports me.'

'I am grateful to the Earth for all these resources that are necessary for my life: the air, the water, the soil.'

'I send my gratitude to the Earth itself from which things grow and from which I eat.'

Your conscious awareness of the gratitude that you bring intentionally to the Earth is a form of giving back—from the heart.

This is a simple practice. We are not saying that everything must be cleared from the mind except this awareness of gratitude. No, we are saying, start lightly. You do not need to take every step with intention, or in silence. Sometimes you may forget, and then you're just walking along. But still you have set your intention, and you can remember, 'Oh, yes, I intend to be planting my gratitude with each step. Oh, yes.' And then you may get distracted, but you are still walking, and that is fine. Even when you are distracted, the intention you're planting is being nourished, fostered, strengthened.

Of course, if you are someone who meditates deeply and does walking meditation, then just add to your silence and your presence the knowing of your gratitude. Yes. It may seem strange that just the act of walking with gratitude is beneficial to the Earth. But as you already know, energies are very powerful. They are what make up the world. The energy with which you do anything has an effect. Even if you do not always see it, you are adding to the energies that are already around you.

So this is our suggestion for a simple act to help heal the Earth, because for most of you, walking is a simple act. For you who cannot walk, who are not able to take steps, you can be aware that you live on the Earth and are part of the Earth. As you sit in your chair, know that gravity is holding you in the chair. And as a part of Earth, you move through the air and take air into your body. Remember that Earth is there for you and be grateful. Send gratitude to the Earth for what is offered, and for what you are able to receive.

That is our message for step one, so to speak.

True gratitude moves from the heart

We want to talk about the healing of the Earth because from our perspective, there is the opportunity now and in the foreseeable future for more and more of those who are incarnated to address the Earth both energetically and in their physical activities.

The physical activities can be of many kinds: planting trees, cleaning up water, protecting endangered species. There are so many things needing help. And there are many groups working on this. In addition, there are many who are now focused on healing energetically. We want to inform those who are interested in energetic healing about techniques and ways of thinking that are most beneficial for the Earth.

Gratitude toward the Earth is an important contribution to the Earth's healing. You may ask, what good is gratitude when there is so much damage, and yet gratitude heals the spirit. Gratitude heals the spirit of the recipient of the gratitude as well as the one who is expressing it. Gratitude is one of those two-way streets. It is not one way. And even though it may be sent out to a specific focus, the energy that is expressed also returns to the one who expressed it. So gratitude is a very powerful energy.

`The effects of that energy are not well expressed by the common use of the word. Gratitude is understood to be about being thankful and appreciative. Those are things that on the surface have to do with politeness. It is polite to say thank you. It is polite to appreciate an effort someone has made. But gratitude is deeper. Gratitude is about knowing, about feeling in the heart—it is not about speech and not about conforming or politeness. It is an energy of the heart, coming from the heart chakra, the energy of love that you carry. Everyone carries this capacity for true gratitude that moves from the heart. You can say, "I am so grateful" and it can be nothing more than politeness or manipulation or many things. But when it comes from the heart, it is pure.

Like everything, the Earth is made up of vibrations. There is a vibratory resonance in every tiny molecule and atom that makes up all the elements and aspects of you and the Earth. And just as with a tuning fork, when you strike a particular chord, that vibration moves out. So when you hit gratitude on your tuning fork for the Earth, that vibration moves through the Earth like the ripples in a pond. And when many people are all sending gratitude, then that beneficial energy amplifies.

Now, we are not saying that as a result, the pollution in the ocean will evaporate. It will not. And we are not saying that when there is more energy for the Earth there will be no more damaging storms, earthquakes, hurricanes, tidal waves, drought. All these things are part of the Earth's struggle for health, balance and well-being, clearing and healing.

So you may not feel an immediate result when you send gratitude to the Earth. If all the resonance and vibrations of gratitude gave the Earth more energy to clear what has been harmed, then there might be more destruction, loss, damage. You might not be grateful for that. That might be a source of sadness, frustration, worry or alarm. But that is on the human scale. On the planetary scale, those kinds of movements can be very beneficial. Because the earth is movement. Creation energy is movement.

Expressing gratitude for the Earth is just one aspect of how those of you in bodies who are aware can be helpful to the Earth. How you think about the Earth matters. We encourage you to think positively. Instead of thinking about pollution, about problems of drought or too much water, about the soil that has been contaminated or areas that have been drained or excavated to extreme, think about the blessings of the elements, of all that arises from the planet's water, air, fire, and earth. Think about the gift of mountains, of soil, of water, of wind and air, of fire, the sun, heat. Be grateful for woods, stones and mountains. Think about the whole. See the planet as a whole. Be grateful for the whole—not just the little part that you are standing on, but the whole.

Even though you may feel much sadness for what has happened to the Earth, that sadness is not so beneficial.

Acknowledge what you feel, all that you see. But also see the beauty. Give your great gratitude for all that has been created and all that is offered. Remember the whole. It made a difference when your technology allowed you to go up and see the planet in its entirety from space. Suddenly there was great appreciation for this beautiful blue ball floating in space. And that attention was very powerful and beneficial for the Earth's vibrations.

We are not saying that in your technological age, you can return to the time when all peoples bowed to the elements of fire and water and gave blessings and created rituals in order to appease the anger of the Earth. We are saying, though, that the vibrational reality of the Earth has been affected by all that has been done on the planet and to the planet without regard to health, without regard to well-being, either for those who are on the Earth or for the planet itself.

So it is time for everyone to invest their energies in healing this planet on which they live. That healing will have physical aspects, but right now it is possible to benefit the Earth on an energetic level. And it is not costly. It is free, but it takes intention, and it takes consistent attention. It takes wanting and choosing to participate in strengthening the health of the Earth.

Deepen your connection with the Earth

We think that it is helpful for everyone to deepen their sense of connection with the Earth. And so, yes, we have spoken about the opening of feet and feeling the energy of the Earth. But connection is also about making a relationship with Earth. It is making a conscious relationship with this planet on which you are embodied. When you enter into a relationship, you wish to learn more about the other. You wish to engage in connecting activities. You wish to share things about yourself with the other. There are so many different aspects of the Earth that everyone can find their path to making relationship with the Earth.

Some are gardeners. They dig in the earth, they plant in the earth. They bring water to what they have planted. They look for the sun to heat the soil and give energy to the seeds. This is a very deep connection with the earth and its cycles and resources. Gardening is a personal relationship with the soil. It is nurturing, fostering, caring. It is being gentle with what is growing. And ultimately, there is a reward of fruits and vegetables, things grown from and with the Earth. And then you can eat this with the additional pleasure of knowing that you grew it with the Earth's support. And this is often the missing component: being grateful to the Earth for what it has allowed you to create, for allowing you to provide for your family, to provide for yourself, to provide for the animals that sneak in and eat the vegetables or the leaves. So gardening can bring closeness with the Earth, but it takes learning, awareness, intention and the deepening of appreciation.

There are also those who build with sensitivity to the environment, as well as sensitivity to the materials they are using and with great appreciation for all the materials that allow them to construct. And then there are those who are simply putting nails or staples into wood. If you are someone who constructs, who builds, even if you are making a bookshelf in your room, there is a way of doing an activity with gratitude because these materials come from the Earth. They may be manufactured, but they are manufactured from materials that come from the Earth. You can be sensitive in realizing that if you are looking at materials that may have brought harm to some aspect of the Earth in their creation, you can choose not to use those materials. Or if you must use such materials, you can do so while sending Earth your gratitude and your wish for its healing. Is not every activity an opportunity to grow in your connection to the Earth?

If you are parachuting from a plane, you are moving through the air, and it is the motion that gives you joy. And although you could not get up high enough to jump out with your parachute without many manufactured things, once you are up there, in the blessing that the environment of air creates, you can look down on the Earth with your heart open.

What we are saying is that whatever you are doing, look at it as a way to deepen your relationship with the Earth. You show the Earth who you are by how you relate to it. Earth gives you gifts; how are you responding? How much are you thanking the Earth? The gifts arrive daily, 24 hours a day, seven days a week, all the days of every month, all the days of every year. How much are you aware of these gifts? There is no greater gift to give than what the Earth gives of itself. The Earth gives you this opportunity to have a body and to live here so that your soul may learn. Well, that is a huge gift. So every day, would it not make sense, throughout the day, to be grateful? To be in relationship and to give thanks and acknowledge the gifts? Acknowledge the way you are using and appreciating the gifts as a gift back to the Earth.

We are not saying that friendships and relationships are transactional. It is not a matter of 'You did that so now I must do something back.' It is not that. It is making a relationship based on love and gratitude. Do you think that the Earth does not know you? Do you think it is too vast to receive your connection? Each of your footsteps, as you walk on the Earth, is noted. Every footstep is an opportunity.

Our message is that in your life one relationship that needs your attention is your relationship with the Earth.

Each person will find their own way to do this; we are saying that this is an important thing to do.

The Earth is a teacher

We want to return to the message of wholeness for the Earth. You understand that any time there is an expression of gratitude to the Earth, it transfers into the Earth and the Earth receives it. The Earth is water, soil, stone, mineral, air, fire. In its physical expression the Earth is all those things: the waters that run deep, the waters on the surface, the fires at the core. Expressions of gratitude, in whatever form, give a gift to the Earth. Planting with the expression of gratitude for the soil, having pleasure and gratitude for the air and the wind when there is a kite flying—all of these small, tiny expressions of gratitude flow to Earth. You could think of it like rain, an energetic rain of gratitude that occurs any time there is a connection to the elements, and gratitude for what the elements teach about power or size or place. All of these expressions move to the Earth and become part of its energy field. The Earth, that large biosphere, is receiving constantly human thoughts, both positive and negative. Every time there is a positive thought, a positive expression, it helps to balance the Earth's energies.

We want to focus now on another aspect of the Earth's purpose. The Earth is not just a place, a location, a reservoir and provider of resources for living things. The Earth is not just here to support life, but to teach life; not just here to give birth to life, but also to teach about how to live. The Earth is a teacher, offering profound wisdom.

Let us talk first about the element of water. The element of water is essential. You know from your experience and your science that the element of water is essential to life. But the element of water is not just a source for drinking or for life to form and reform. Water is also a primary element for teaching.

What does water teach? Water teaches flow. It teaches change. And it teaches about the lack of those things. What happens when there is no movement? When things stagnate? What happens when things are contained and not allowed to move? Movement is one of the core aspects water teaches: the power of slow, gentle movement and the misfortune of flow being denied, prevented, interrupted.

Even when water is not moving, life forms are still using the water. Things are still being born, but over time there is more corruption to the living things within the water that is not refreshed. Pollution also has negative effects on the life forms within the water and the life forms that depend on the water. But when the water can move freely, water has very powerful cleansing abilities. When the water can move, time will heal the pollution. Although it will not heal the life forms that are damaged in the interim, water has its own mechanisms for healing within it as well as in connection to other elements, because it is part of the whole interconnected system.

The Earth provides the sand, the soil, the heat from the fire of the sun and the heat that rises from the core of the Earth, and the winds that pick up the water and cleanse it before it moves back down to the Earth. By focusing on wholeness, we want to offer an increased understanding of what the Earth itself is able to do and how the parts fit together.

The energy of love

Today what we wish to address with you is the energy of love. Yes. That word has so much connected to it, so much projected onto it. But we are not speaking about the word. We are speaking about the *frequency*, the frequency that is associated on our plane with that word. It is a very high frequency, while the word is often used on your plane in a way that is very low. Love is withheld. It is manipulated. It is about transactions, and complicated emotions. But that is not the love of which we speak.

When you connect with your own soul energy, you raise your vibration up to touch this aspect of your being. In whatever way you experience this connection, there is a very strong core of love within the combination of frequencies that are your soul. That frequency of love is a part of you in this embodiment. Whether it remains hidden away or shining forth, it is within you.

We have said that to walk upon the Earth with awareness, making each step one of love, is an important act. We understand that to do this with every step is not realistic. You know how central your breath is to your life, but you are not aware of every breath. However, the breath changes, becoming deeper and more nourishing, when you are aware of it. In this way, when you are aware of your love for the Earth, and your love of this life that the Earth is giving you, then that too brings more nourishment to the Earth. Just as you do not have to remember to breathe, you do not have to remember to express love with each step, only to but remind your being that it is your intention to express love of the Earth— to express not just gratitude but also love.

Find that place in the heart chakra, that place of love as free, unconditional giving—not as transaction, not as exchange, not as need. That place of free, unconditional loving is within everyone. Everyone has that capability. Though it remains hard to access or closed for some, it is nevertheless there. For those who may have problems expressing love toward other humans, maybe there is the way to express it toward animals. Maybe there is a way to express it to the Earth: to living things, to trees, to flowers. Each one of you can find that place within you that is capable of unconditional, freely given love. Find that place, find where it currently has expression, and expand that expression to include in your love the Earth as a whole.

Perhaps life has been hard. But nevertheless, the Earth has given you the resources to live; it has given you the sun and the soil and the growing things and the air. When you plant your feet on the Earth and look around, you see the growing things; when you look up, you see the sun; and you breathe the Earth's air at every moment. Becoming more aware of this, find first the gratitude and then find the love, because the Earth is in desperate need. The Earth does not ask for love, but welcomes, welcomes, welcomes it.

When you send your gratitude, the Earth absorbs that and it is very comforting. When you express and send forth your love of the Earth—of its elements, of that which it supports—the vibration of your love raises the energies of the Earth. When you are in full expression of love, your own energies expand. You are larger, you are lighter, you are lifted up. Just so, the more love that is expressed to the Earth, the more the Earth's energy is lifted.

That lifting is very much needed right now. When you are feeling depressed or burdened, it is very hard to act wisely. This low vibration is very constraining and limiting. But when you are lifted up, then the energy for activity, the energy for hope, the energy for possibilities also expands. This is what you are assisting when you focus intentionally on expressing your love for the Earth, and programing your being to be expressing that even when it is not in your conscious mind. You are contributing to raising the vibration of the Earth. And that is very important at this time.

Act from love

Our focus is very much on healing; we send healing energies to the Earth and all beings and all things on the Earth. Our interest and what we see as possible is the expansion of the consciousness of those who already care about healing and the healing of the planet to understand the greater whole, not in their mind, but in their heart and in their energies.

We want those who are working on the ocean waters to understand that, yes, cleaning out the plastic or cleaning out the oil is a very important task. It is duty. It is responsibility. It is very important. But when they are doing these things, we want them to have a consciousness of the greater whole: that in doing this one act, they are assisting the whole of the planet because when that is the energy with which an action is taken, the vibration is different. The way it echoes and moves out into the planetary system is different.

If you pick up a piece of trash and you are thinking, 'How disgusting, that person was not thoughtful, how rude,' then it is the energy of your disgust, your dislike, that moves with the action. When the consciousness and the energies of sadness, anger, loss, pain, suffering—when that is part of how the work is done, then the energy of loss—more pain, more suffering—is communicated emotionally and those waves go out and that is not beneficial.

But if you pick up the trash and you think, 'The Earth is so beautiful, I am happy to remove this piece of paper, which is in the way of my seeing the beauty here. I will put it in a place where it will not further harm the Earth, perhaps in the landfill where it can go back to the Earth.' When that is the consciousness, more beneficial energies are sent out.

We are seeing the image of the people who care about the forest and the trees, the tree huggers. When they express their love of trees, their love of the Earth, their love of the roots of the trees, their love of the community of the trees, that is so beneficial, that is so helpful. That supports the larger healing of the Earth because the energy that is being sent out is one of love and healing and embrace. That is health.

When those who love the forests are focused on hating the people who log the trees or want to cut forests to build houses, and they are angry, fearful and saddened, sometimes feeling the loss that has not yet happened for them, then those are the energies that spread out—and those energies are not beneficial.

The point in our teaching is to be conscious of the whole. Do not fear that you must understand the complexity of the Earth's components, or of how things are healed. Instead, it is important to understand about opening up consciousness and awareness so that the intention with which each act is performed in the service of the Earth carries with it the vibration of further healing for the Earth.

The Earth needs your love

Those of you on the planet are seeing and hearing and knowing every day of the disruptions: fires, floods, droughts, famine, disease, pollution of the air and waters and land. You see both the damage done to the Earth and its actions to cleanse and heal itself. We want you to know the Earth is always expressing from the essence of creation and love toward growth and evolution. While what you see may evoke sadness and anger, what the Earth needs now is your love. What the Earth needs is your joy and gratitude for all that the Earth has created and all that it has given you. The Earth is your home and has been very generous in providing everything that you need to have a body and live on the planet. It is understandable that you speak of Mother Earth when you think of what has been given. The Earth is incredibly creative and generously loving in your human terms.

You do not need to be in awe-inspiring mountains or deep in the most beautiful of forests to appreciate the beauty Earth offers. Can you not see the beauty of the seed that pushes through the cement to grow? Each and every living thing, in its own way, has its own incredible beauty. Look for it. Find it. Love it and send your gratitude to the Earth. Every thought, every feeling that you have about the Earth goes into the Earth and its energetic field.

Right now, you can help to raise the vibration of the Earth and in doing so you help the Earth to continue to evolve, to ascend to a higher energetic dimension. We ask that you send your blessings (yes, the blessings you send are sacred and count mightily) to the Earth from your heart, that all may be benefited.

Wholeness and healing

The healing of the Earth occurs through healing the people who walk upon the Earth, the creatures that walk upon the Earth, that which grows upon the Earth, and also that which makes up the planet itself. The healing occurs from the very deep core, up through the layers of the Earth, up through the pores and the feet of those who walk upon the Earth, and up through the roots of what grows into the Earth. So our interest, as you can see, is very broad and deep. The opportunity to engage with those on the Earth who are aware and interested in the whole notion of healing—healing the Earth and connecting all healing to the healing of the Earth—is important.

We wish to expand awareness of how the healing of one who walks on the Earth is part of healing the Earth itself.

It is one whole, you understand. The Earth is not all these separate bits. Although the separate bits come and go, arise and die, form and unform, yet that great movement, that great cycle of energy exchange, is all one thing. Many things make up this big whole. And yes, you can imagine that when we are looking at a universe, it is also one whole. Everything begins with the notion of wholeness. Everything, *everything*, is part of a greater whole. More than you see through your telescopes is part of the whole. And each whole is itself made up of smaller and smaller and smaller whole things. Each wholeness contributes itself as part of the expression of the larger and larger wholes to be expressed.

The Earth is a force of creation energies. These are visible to you, palpable to you. You receive life force energies from the Earth. It is a misconception to think that you can draw from the Earth's energies and that those energies are automatically replenished. No. When you are drawing energy to you from the Earth, it is important that you also give back to the Earth. The Native American and other indigenous people's traditions of offering to the Earth prayers of gratitude, or a gift of something valued, a gift that has grown on the Earth, these practices were rooted in wisdom. Each time there is gratitude, there is an energy that moves back to the Earth. When you have received a gift from the Earth, you return energy to the Earth. You can offer beneficial energy to the Earth in many ways, but sending your gratitude is a simple, straightforward way.

We know that there will be upheavals. The Earth is wounded and must express the wounds so that they can be healed. You know, when there is too much sickness inside a person, there are ways that the sickness needs to be expressed and excised—it could be through throwing up, medication to minimize the disease, surgeries to remove something that cannot otherwise be minimized, radiation to reduce a sickness, which sometimes then causes other harms. The Earth has its own ways of getting rid of that which is making the Earth ill, to use your medical term. But it is better if you think of the Earth as wounded. There are wounds and bruises. To help the Earth heal will take time. It takes patience. It takes deep intention. It is helpful to understand the healing process.

Each time we are working on healing a person we are really working on helping them align their energies for their own healing. We provide energy: an infusion of energy, an infusion of intention, an infusion of direction that can be used by the person's higher self to facilitate that which comes next. It is not always possible that what comes next is perfect health or complete healing, or even partial healing. Sometimes the energy that we provide is used to simply cushion the distress because it is not in the soul's interest for that person to attain healing at this time, in this way. It is important to understand that when we send healing energies, it is without expectation of specific outcomes. It is very important, because it is easy for those serving as healers and those seeking healing to be misled into your dichotomy of successful/unsuccessful or correct/incorrect when it comes to healing.

Healing is very complex in terms of the physical, the emotional, the energetic, the social. There are so many levels of history and future and present, all connected to anyone to whom we might send healing energies; we can see potentials but really we do not know what aspects of the being the energy is going to infuse. In some ways that is beneficial. What we can know is that the energies that we are sending for the purposes of healing are sent with the intention of support, release and healing. How the higher consciousness of the person to whom they are sent uses those energies, allows those energies in, is not up to us. It is up to the person, although the person does not always have to be involved for the energies to move into them and to provide some benefit. But the energies move to a person with most effectiveness when the higher aspect of the person, what you might call the higher self, is engaged and supporting. We send our energies only with permission and with protections for the person in place.

When we are focused on healing a person, we are also working towards healing the planet. Each one of you is part of the wholeness of Earth. Your way of being is part of the Earth's Being. When human beings walk on the Earth with greater alignment, awareness, connection, health and well-being, the Earth too enjoys greater alignment and health.

The Earth is one interconnected whole

An important part of the story is this idea of the Earth being in its own process of healing and how that manifests. When you reflect on the healing of the Earth, you think about how an individual seeks healing for something that is wrong. Sometimes that means something must be expelled, removed or cut out. Sometimes it means that there is a mending, a stitching together needed. Sometimes it means that healing occurs from the inside out, and other times from the outside in. There are so many different ways that the body tries to cope with things that go wrong with it—disease and imbalances arising from environmental, genetic, emotional, and psychosocial conditions. When things are out of balance, when aspects of the planet—the waters, air, core, layers of soil, rocks, minerals—are experiencing dis-ease, then there is a systemic response because, like you, the Earth is one interconnected whole.

The Earth has complex responses. Depending on the nature of the dis-ease, there are repercussions, which you may experience as alarming. These are nothing more than the Earth doing what it can to bring its being into health, into alignment, into wholeness for the well-being of all. As we have been saying, it is not just the round ball of the Earth and the atmosphere surrounding the planet that is affected. All that lives, walks, swims, flies on the Earth, all that grows from the Earth is part of the planet's expression and being. When the planet is out of balance and has many dis-eases to address, then the people and everything on the planet are impacted because there is insufficient healthy energy to easily surround and heal all of the growing things on the Earth (and by growing things, yes, we include all the mountains and the rivers, all that is).

One can understand then that weather patterns, earthquakes, ocean temperatures, volcanic eruptions, and floods, for example, are both evidence of dis-ease as well as manifestations of attempts to heal, to come back into balance so that creation energies can express the next steps in the Earth's evolutionary growth as a place supporting the potential for humanity's expansion into higher consciousness. The Earth is an entity of enormous energy whose evolution and purposes are tied to those of humanity. The Earth's actions, even as they now have some negative consequences for humans, are not an expression of punishment or anger but are part of the healing necessary for both the Earth and human beings. As you know in your own experiences with healing, there is often pain that accompanies movement back into health. This is true for the Earth and humanity, now going through this time of necessary healing together.

Many layers for healing

There are levels of healing, and each level of healing is a process of change. When you have a cut, your skin is changed, and then it changes again when it begins to heal. It goes through a process of changing at the cellular level, as the new cells come in. New skin is created in layers, because your body is made up of layers. In cases where the physical disruption is greater, causing distress and remaining unhealed, not only the physical body is affected. There may also be anger, depression, sadness, and discouragement and these feelings weigh on the self and create an even larger burden, an emotional wounding that also requires healing.

When you have an emotional wounding, there is no physical manifestation on the skin or in the organs, but nevertheless there is a wound, and that wound is in the emotional body, and that emotional body has its place in your energetic field. Your emotional body is not inside your skin. You feel your feelings but they do not have an organ. No, they do not have an organ, but they are part of you, and they have a place in your etheric field. And so when an emotional wound is healing, you understand it through your mental processes, though the actual healing occurs in your etheric emotional body, in your energetic field. When you are wounded emotionally and remain unhealed, the wound can affect your physical body as well, because your energetic field has been affected, and you are one whole, not separate disunited parts. So healing is always about healing all the layers, healing the whole.

Just like your body, the Earth has layers that go down to the physical core, as well as the layers that are the Earth's energetic field. When there is a physical wounding to the Earth, there is also that wounding in the field. And when there are energetic impulses from those who are on the Earth and those impulses are at a lower level—the impulses of greed, for example, or the impulses of hate, the impulses of destruction, of unkindness, all these lower-level feelings, thoughts, actions—not only is the physical Earth affected, but also the layers of the Earth's energetic field. So just as you can carry a wound that weighs you down with a lower vibration, the Earth has been burdened by very heavy, lower, dense vibrations. Although you like your blue skies and your light, fluffy clouds, those of you on two legs in human embodiment have created a dense, dark cloud of energies that surround and oppress the Earth.

There is the need, for those who can, to assist the physical earth—the resources, trees, mountains, waters, biodiversity—all those things of creation that are part of the Earth's energies. And as we have said, when this work is done with compassion, rather than with anger or sadness, the Earth is aided. Compassion is anchored in love, and love is what is needed.

When one is doing hands-on work with love, kindness, and open-heartedness, then two things are achieved at the same time. It helps the physical Earth, and it also moves higher vibrations into the Earth's field, so that the dense, lower energy can be dissipated. Love always cleanses and transforms. But it cannot just be at the level of thought. It must be the true frequency of love.

You can think, 'Oh, I love that,' but there is no higher frequency behind the words. But when you truly open to the expanded and generous state of love, that is indeed a higher frequency. When that genuine expression of love of the Earth joins with other expressions of love for the Earth, the result is more lightness penetrating that dense cloud of lower vibrations and countering them with love, appreciation, respect and compassion for the Earth. That is very beneficial.

When there is genuine, open-hearted love of one another, that also helps to penetrate some of the dense energies surrounding the Earth, since the Earth's field is affected not only by what is done to the Earth, but also by what is done on the Earth. The density around the Earth comes from the energetic fields of all who are upon the Earth. And at present there is so much sadness, hate, and anger. When you have a collection of beings with these low-frequency vibrations they seep out and accumulate, resulting in more density for everyone. It affects individuals in their own being and as a collective, and it affects the Earth's energetic field.

So to be a healer of the Earth, one must also be a healer of one's own energetic being. It is not simple. And it is an ongoing responsibility. There are many now called to attend to this, because if enough of those of you who are embodied work with those of us who are not embodied—if we join together, we have the opportunity to lift that dense, lower-vibration cloud that surrounds the Earth, enabling those who can to open their own beings to a higher vibration. When there is a change in the overall frequency surrounding the Earth, there will be those who rush to be embodied on the Earth. At the same time, with that higher frequency open, there will be those who rush to leave, who no longer can be in their skin, because there is no fit.

Disruption at every layer of the Earth

There is disruption in the patterns the world is experiencing, particularly focused on climatic changes, but also what is happening with the animals. There is disruption at every layer of the Earth and among all the things that are part of the Earth: the fish, the animals, the birds, the insects, the amphibians, and the humans—everything is being affected in a way that increases disruption. Patterns that have existed for a long time are being disrupted and changed in a way that is striking or violent or completely inexplicable. There are species that are not behaving in their normal ways, just as there are species that are moving into full extinction. And as your biodiversity lessens, the concentration of what remains is no longer within the parameters of healthy expression, healthy creation. More disruption then arises among more aspects of living things.

We know you have this phrase 'endgame.' But this is not an endgame. It is not a game. It is a life cycle that stretches over much more than millennia. When there is this kind of change, out of destruction can come creation—out of what is lost can come what is new. When there is a forest fire, the mature trees die and new life comes. But at this point in the cycle, given the depletion of Earth energies, that renewal will not be as it has been.

In a sense, either there is a collapsing or there is an ascension. There is either a caving in or there is a rising up. And that point of choice is not localized within what you would call a year or 10 years. As decisions are made, as energies are expressed moment by moment, the balance moves either toward collapse or toward ascending.

You can compare what is happening to a human being living their life. The person is affected by everything that surrounds them and all the decisions they make. If poor decisions have been made, the health of this person is not so good and their energies degrade. Or perhaps good decisions are made, and new energies come in, leading to a renewal of life force and beneficial energies. And out of this, more decisions are made, and more energy comes in, resulting in more moments where love, kindness and compassion arise and grow, and there is an ascending, an enhancement of the being. So, too, with the planet. The planet's energies are dependent upon what is flowing to it, what is done to it and the energy sent into its field.

Right now there is an opportunity to increase the higher frequencies surrounding the planet—the frequencies that determine the experience of all the forms of Earth and all the forms that live and exist upon the Earth. This is a moment where the simple act of choosing to send love and light to the Earth—to the people of the Earth, but also to the energy surrounding the Earth—is in itself a beneficial act.

You can do it before you get up in the morning. You can do it while you brush your teeth. It does not need to be a 30-minute meditation or even a five-minute meditation. It needs to be an intention—an intention to send that energy up and out to benefit the planet and all that is upon it. This is something that everyone can do every day. And so why not do it? Even if you cannot imagine that it will truly help, why not do it anyway?

Wholeness is a state of being

We want to connect healing more deeply to the understanding of wholeness. Often when healing is occurring, there is the limited notion of it occurring in a particular part of the body in a particular person, and that it is for a disease, a discomfort, a specific physical occurrence. And while that may be happening, that is not the only thing that is happening, because at the same moment, whenever there is a physical disturbance—a disease, a bruise, a discomfort, inflammation—yes, when those things are occurring, there is also a disturbance to the etheric body, to the energy field.

When there is a problem physically, it also manifests in the energy field. It manifests within the energy field to different degrees as a weakness in terms of the whole, which carries through to other beings or the greater whole of the Earth. For each person, each animal, each living thing that is carrying a damage, a disease, or other manifestation of a problem, all of those collectively affect the larger whole. You can also think of the way it happens with a person when there is a physical illness of some kind and then the person's emotions are affected by the stress or the fears, the pain of the physical illness. The mental health, the thought processes and the beliefs taking root in the person's energy field are also constrained, contracted, affected, limited. When this happens, the connection to higher vibrations, to spirit, is impeded. In that sense, one thing occurring in the body causes a ripple effect through the whole of the being because now perhaps the person is distracted, their life purpose is impeded and has been removed from consciousness. And then you can see the whole process of increasing contraction of energies. And when all aspects of this being are in contraction, what is there to be contributed to the healing of the self, to others, to the world, to the healing of the greater whole? Less and less.

We are here to remind you that healing is never about one aspect. You cannot work on just one level because what is happening on one level affects all the others. It is always about the whole. When you are talking about holistic medicine, you are talking about a medicine that is perhaps more organic in its creation and that takes into account that there are emotions and spirit. That is a step forward. But we want you to take another step. We want you to understand that it is not just what is happening for the person, not just what is happening in their mental processes and emotional processes connected to their physical expression. It is healing on all the etheric levels and beyond. It is about healing that goes into the planet, up to the heavens. You could say that it is about being whole and in wholeness, which automatically flows to the planet on which you are residing. And it is healing for others who are connected to you, who will also experience the energy of wholeness. The energetic impact of wholeness is to promote more wholeness.

We are trying to remove this notion of duality and separateness. We want to talk about what it means to be whole. When you join with a group and make a circle with the intention of bringing together the energies of that circle, that field of energy is expanded or constrained by what each member can contribute in terms of the flow of energies. When there are weaknesses because of unhealed aspects held in the fields of those present, then the group's energy is smaller. But when those present bring greater levels of healthy energies, then the whole of the group is healthy and the energies are impressive when joined. Of course, on your plane of existence it would be rare to find a group of people who had moved through all their healing—physical, emotional, mental and spiritual—and existed as a perfect whole in connection with the greater All. Your planet has not provided the foundation for this way of being.

In any gathering of people, everyone's field of energy is present. Do you not find some groups uncomfortable even if nothing is being said or done that 'bothers' you? Imagine all that is being contributed by each of those who are present. Imagine the Earth who must support every being's energy field as well as their actions as they affect the Earth and other living things. This is why the healing of the Earth begins with the healing of human beings. What we are suggesting is that expanded awareness of wholeness and awareness of all the layers of healing are important steps for the future of the planet and humanity.

Wholeness is not perfection

We return to our subject of when an individual is wounded. We are focused mainly on physical damage: a disease, a disruption to the healthy functioning of an organ, or a misuse of muscles, tendons, ligaments that then become strained, overstretched, and not functioning healthily. A weakness is created when there is dis-ease—when there is an interdiction of the normal, healthy functioning of anything in the human body system. As we have said, the weakness then is not just in the body, but in all the energies that move out from the body that are part of the energetic whole, which is in its turn part of a larger whole, which is part of a larger whole and so forth.

When the physical healing that is undertaken creates other problems, then even if there is a healing of one part, there is damage elsewhere. And so the weakness is simply moved. The purpose of healing is to have wholeness. Approaches to healing that harm one aspect of the physical being to correct another aspect of the physical being are not part of holistic healing, by which we mean the addressing the interconnectedness of all. We are talking about healing the whole, going all the way down into the Earth, because the Earth is part of the holistic connection, the whole being. Every being on the planet and their energies make up, we could say, a molecule of the Earth's healing and wholeness. So for the Earth to be fully healed and whole, every being, everything on the planet would need to be whole. But that is not really the goal, for the energy of creation is always movement, change, transformation.

Movement toward greater healing and wholeness is a formidable task for a human being. Nevertheless, moments of great healing and wholeness are possible for an incarnated being. Your sense of time is not part of the larger reality.

From our perspective great changes and great healing can occur very quickly. From our perspective, healing can move back through what you think of as the past as well as forward into what you see as the future.

You are not here with the goal of perfection, because if there were complete perfection, what would be the point? Creation is not about perfection. Creation is about the opportunity for expression, the opportunity to experiment, the opportunity to explore. So you could ask, why are we focused on this notion of wholeness if perfection, which is how you view wholeness, is not the purpose?

This is complicated to explain. We will talk first about the difference between wholeness and perfection. Perfection is not a concept that is part of our vocabulary. It is not a meaningful concept to us. Because what is perfection? Is a smooth surface perfection for surfaces? No, because many surfaces, in their right expression, have bumps, or perhaps they even have holes. They have texture. So smooth might be chosen for one expression, but it is not perfection. And then if that is what you think of as perfection, what is the point of doing more? What is the point of going forward to try to re-create the perfection you thought you had already achieved? You can see that it is difficult for us to grasp this notion of perfection as an ideal, as even as an idea. We think it is not a useful concept, but rather one that leads souls astray all the time. So let us drop this notion of perfection.

Wholeness is not perfection. Wholeness is a state of being that runs through the physical and energetic levels associated with you. When your awareness takes you into the Earth and into your soul and beyond, up to the heavens and the other energies, when you are holding all of that in your awareness, then your understanding of the meaning of wholeness expands. And in expanding your understanding of wholeness, you automatically increase your own wholeness, which expands the opportunity to heal weaknesses that may start in the etheric areas of your being and move into the body or may start in the body and move out through your energy fields. Your ability to heal those weaknesses and strengthen the energy of your wholeness is expanded.

Are you understanding this? It is essential to connect your awareness not just to the physical body, but also deeply to Earth and outward, through your etheric fields and up to higher vibrations, to your soul, to spirit. When you hold this sense of awareness while you focus on healing some weakness, whether it is physical, mental, emotional, or spiritual, part of the concrete expression of your being or part of your energy field, then you are able to bring in more energy to heal that weakness.

At the same time, you are able to expand the healing to move through all the layers—down into the Earth and up through spirit. All that healing then moves out and strengthens the larger wholes of which you are a part.

You are a very small, very tiny but important component of all that is on the Earth. Every molecule, every atom that makes up anything that exists in your world is important. When they change, what is created changes. You, as a tiny part of the Earth and the galaxies, make a difference. Your being makes a difference. The health of your being contributes to the health of the ever greater whole. The health of every tree, every four-legged, the winged ones, all those in the sea—all of these energies make up this whole that you think of as the Earth. You tend to think you walk upon the Earth, but not that you are a part of it. But we are saying that you are not separate.

Many like the idea that "all is one." Well, "all is one" means that every time you take a step on the Earth, you are taking a step on something you are deeply a part of. And how you are in your own well-being, in your own wholeness, affects how the Earth is in its health and wholeness. And the Earth's health and wholeness is part of a larger unit of existences. Think of the universe, think of galaxies. All one great whole.

This is not a simple idea. We reduce it to a simple idea, "all is one," because the mind can take that in more easily, in a limited way. But we see that this as a moment when there is the possibility to understand more deeply what this means. To be on this planet now is to be present when there is great energy and support for healing into greater wholeness. This is a time to take advantage of the opening for change, an opening for greater healing and greater awareness.

Destabilization of old forms

Human activities across the planet are creating increasing levels of insecurity and destabilization. It was never that the foundations were stable. The planetary vibrations do not encourage such stability. We have spoken of the disconnection that is part of your belief systems, which are all based upon many different divisions and dualities and separations and hierarchies—which all create not the strength of unity, but the weaknesses of disconnections.

The more things are disconnected, the more there is insecurity, because there is a yearning in humankind and indeed across life forms for a sense of place and connection. When places are destabilized because of Earth changes or violent, greedy human interventions, then there cannot be connection to place. And then there is disconnection among people. In a world where there has never been great stability, there have been illusions strong enough to hold a center, to hold a sense of connection. But it has never been what you would call real. It has been on the surface, and surfaces are easily disrupted.

What is connection? When it is understood to be technological, it is not an energetic connection. It is not that technology cannot be a support, but without an acknowledgment of where the real connection exists, it is just a different sort of illusion.

You are in a situation now of insecurity and destabilization, and this is not going to improve. But some of what is creating the destabilization of old forms and the insecurities of those attached to the old forms are the new forms that are attempting to break through and create new possibilities of connection for humankind, for the planet. Part of the new energy surrounds experiences of those who are denying the category that they have been placed in. There is resistance to being forced into a way of seeing the self that creates separation within the individual and from other individuals.

For example, when one is what you are calling non-binary, refusing a binary category to belong to, they are asserting the reality of their own energetic truth that they are not just one thing. And what they may choose to express may vary. Each time you see news about those who are choosing not to label themselves in a binary way, you can see that as part of this new energy, a different vibration, which encompasses without dividing and separating.

We want you to experience the difference between when you understand what is arising from your own fullness of being, and when you, in your more limited ego self, want to judge, assert your opinions or understanding, and challenge changes to cultural norms. Notice those very different states of being. The ego self often trusts the brain more than the heart and even seeks to hide the knowing of the fuller self. But your knowing is not limited to what arises from your brain activity. See what happens if you intend to let your ideas flow to and through your heart before they move into expression.

When your awareness comes from an ego perspective, your expressed energies have lower, denser vibrations. Even if you are making a beneficial point for others to hear, the energy that is expressed is what will have the most powerful impact.

When you speak from the heart, from a place of deep understanding, connection and knowing, a different energy is expressed. You might judge and want to improve on your words if they were played back for you, but the meaning occurred in the energies that you were sending out with whatever those words were. It is the energy that is important, that is where the connection happens.

An escalation of conflict

As we are speaking it is the beginning of your new calendar year. We wish to add a further message about what is arising for the planet and what is arising for everyone, though there will be many different individual experiences. We would say that our message will hold true for several years to come.

There is an escalation of the conflicts that have been allowed in the vibration of this planet. This escalation will give rise to even more fear, even more worry. It will be unsettling, deeply unsettling. Those who are ready for change, who themselves wish to tune to a vibration that supports harmony, universal love, and the experience of oneness will find more room for those aspirations of peace, harmony and connection to be expressed. What you will see as escalating conflicts will bring forward a deeper need for the countervailing energies of love and connection with the greater whole that each of you is and that each of you is one with. Even more humans will seek to express peace and to express love because that is what is yearned for in the face of what you will think of as troubling times.

There is also an escalation of planetary response, both to the movement toward higher vibrations and to the misuse and depletions of what the Earth has provided. The Earth itself will bring disruptions to some of the resources and physical matter that you may take for granted. These disruptions, whether they are of water flooding or fire burning or the Earth moving, will cause even more fear to arise. It is important that everyone who has a sense of the possibility of the Earth's ascension to a higher dimension understand that the traumatic events that erupt within the Earth's elements and forms and movements are all part of the clearing out. All are part of the unsettling of what is, to allow the opening to what may be.

You know from your own histories that pioneers—those who are in the front waves of something new—have difficult times. The road is not clearly marked, or the road may not even exist. But in this case, the energy pathways that lead to change do exist. It is a matter of joining them, connecting with them, knowing that you are one with them. There is nothing that exists that you are not connected to. When you open to acknowledging your connection to the energetic movements of ascension within your own being, within your soul's being, within groups of souls, within the whole, then the movement of all the ascension energies overall are expanded.

When there is movement and change, there is often resistance that comes from fear. What is the counter to fear? Love. So love the changes. See what is occurring on the Earth through your heart and your sense of connection to the oneness. Definitely feel compassion for those who are in harm's way. Definitely offer kindness to those who are hurt or afraid, but do not join the fear. Do not join the worry. Instead, join the love.

We understand that this is very difficult. And there will be moments when your own fear will arise. But if you are aware of and watching out for your own fear, you may be able to offer yourself the antidote of your greater self's knowing. In doing this, you assist your own Being, your soul and the planet, in moving toward a greater expression of love, peace, harmony, kindness, and compassion—all those things that hearts and souls yearn to know.

Of course, you must also know all the other experiences—fear, sadness, greed, anger, separation, judgment—all those things that the planetary vibration allows. They are all teachers offering pathways back to the expansion of the light. All learning results in expanded light and the light within you is your connection to the Divine source. It is always there for you.

The impetus of evolution is a positive one

When you look up at the sky and feel the sun's warmth on your face, you feel grateful for the light, for the warmth. You are grateful to have this experience and this warming, welcoming, uplifting sensation. How often do you look up at the shining sun and feel depressed? Much more often you look up at the shining sun and you feel uplifted, grateful, happy. Perhaps even secure. In right proportion the sun causes and supports growth.

But at the same time, in your world, the sun is also a source of things that are not welcomed. The sun's rays come through your weakened atmospheric layers and can cause damage to the skin and disease. The sun, when there is no respite, can cause drought and then lack of food and resources for supporting life.

As the Earth attempts to continue to provide beneficial resources for all, it is important that you bring your awareness of the greater whole. That you bring your own gratitude for what the Earth has created, and gratitude for what the Earth has withstood, along with your inner knowing that the Earth's evolution and that of humans is in a continuing process.

The impetus of evolution is a positive one. The Earth, in its wholeness, is more than just a physical planet with an atmosphere. Just as you have potentials and purposes and a connection to your soul, so does the Earth have potentials and purposes for its creation energies. In addition to all the scientifically identified physical fields, Earth also has its own connection to the larger web of creation energies. The Earth's wholeness is different because it is a wholeness that is planetary and includes the solar systems and galaxies, which are all entities, emerging from and connected to the energies of creation. In this context, Earth is also a young planet, just as humans are a young species.

The changes that have been wrought by abuse, misunderstanding, greed, and inattention have damaged the Earth and therefore damaged living things on the Earth, impeding the Earth's evolution. There has been so much damage, from which certain aspects of the Earth and living things will not recover. At the same time, the energy that is rising to carry forward the potential for the Earth's growth and for the light-filled expansion of living things is that of grace.

Think of a state of grace as a place from which living things might experience, communicate, share, interact. Imagine if each individual were filled with Divine grace and moved out into the world with that vibration, interacting with others from that vibration, looking at the world and looking at others from that connection with Divine grace.

For most of you it is usually easier to meditate and connect with spirit and with your deeper, truer self when you are in a time and place devoted to that activity. Most of you, when you leave these moments of connection, re-enter a world where the energies and experiences that nourish you are not only unacknowledged, but impeded.

What if instead, out in the world, you were met by the energies that reinforced your own sense of love, Divine grace, and the expansion of light? That is the potential future. There would still be learning. There would still be things that were uncomfortable because all energies, even within a general vibration, have different, shall we say, hues. And so on that spectrum, some will be much more comfortable, some will be somewhat less comfortable. But how different would your days be if the base were one of a shared knowing of Divine grace and Divine love?

It is very difficult to describe the potential of what may be, using your words. To understand what we mean, imagine dropping into the energies of your own expanded soul-connected Self. That is the possibility for all embodied humankind in the future. And that is what you are being asked to choose to support. The planet is seeking to evolve to be a place for that state of being.

It is all about choice. What future do you wish to choose, for future embodiments, for yourself and for others? For the essence of the planet? And what might arise from the potential future to which you are being asked to lend your energies and support? In a sense, we are asking you to sign up to support the potential of the planet and its potential future energies, and the potential future of humankind living and learning within a higher vibrational field.

Evolution of the human template

You have asked us if we can put the concept of ascension, the evolution of the Earth and humanity, into a more straightforward explanation. It is difficult for us to translate our understanding into your words. The many different vibrations, dimensions, energies, planes, frequencies—all those words are available to try to describe a very, very complex fluid structure. While there are differences, there is a core, a thread of connection running through all the layers and dimensions, that exists in whatever realm and in form or non-form.

Let us try to put the idea of ascension in very concrete terms. When you were conceived, the seed and the egg connected and there began to be change, growth. When you were born, the internal unfolding process continued. In plants, animals, in all the kingdoms there is this process of ongoing change. And as things grow, old forms, shapes, sizes, constructions, fade away as new shapes, sizes, cells, tissues form. Unless there are disruptions, there is always the letting go of what was and the moving forward into new growth.

This process is not only true on the physical side, the body. It is also true in terms of mental and emotional learning, growth, change. Your ideas change, and when they change, the old ideas fade away. They are overtaken by new ideas. Emotions, too, are ephemeral—one emotion goes away and a new emotion takes its place. You have opportunities for learning about different expressions and to experience an array of possible emotions. All of this is part of the ongoing change and development of the human being.

What you learn at different ages is very different. You replace how you used to move with how you now move. All of these changes are part of your personal evolution, we could say, from a fertilized egg in the womb to a grown, aging human being. That process of change and learning does not stop until you let the body go. The body disappears and then you are in a form without a body, you are energy without a body.

Now think about a larger, more complex evolution, that of the human template—a template for existing in form that evolved to be the thinking, ensouled being. What the human being was capable of in the earliest of times has evolved. What was considered the appropriate way to get nourishment and food has changed dramatically. The organization of communities has changed over and over again. The potential expressions of the human have changed as there has continued to be growth in the capacity of the human to travel, to think, to dream, to understand.

Now, when you look across your globe, you see humanity existing in very fractured ways. Even with all the global communications, there is a fracturing, with deep divisions and rivalries of nations, tribes and identities. And when you look at what is, you think, where does this go? What is next for humanity? Will there be more division, more separateness, more war, more greed, more privileging of the needs and wants of those who have the most? Will corporations as entities be valued as more important than the humans who are part of those entities?

It is the same for the Earth. The Earth has gone through and continues to go through changes of its concrete being: the shapes and movements of earth masses and waters, the air and the fire in the core. There is now much concern about what has been depleted from the Earth, not just in resources, but also in the biodiversity that forms the whole. Earth is one whole. Humans are not just the abusers and the preservers of the Earth's resources in their actions that harm or help the Earth. They are part of the atmosphere of Earth. It is not just human actions, but also your thoughts and emotions that are part of the fabric of the Earth. You see everything as concrete. We see everything as energies. Your thoughts are energies. Your emotions are energies. It all moves out from you. You have what you think of as the atmosphere of Earth. But we are saying that the atmosphere of Earth is much more than that. Everything, including every human, contributes to the atmosphere of Earth. And that atmosphere is either one that allows or suppresses growth. The atmosphere allows for healing or suppresses healing. The purpose of Earth is not to devolve and end. The purpose of Earth is to be a place that continues to evolve, a place where humans can grow and learn and thrive.

Now, for humans to continue to grow and thrive there is the need for change. Since the inception of the planet and humanity, it has always been intended that the Earth and humanity would grow to more refined levels of being, by which we mean less dense, less heavy, less separated, more able to experience connection. This is the process of ascension to a higher vibration of being.

As growth and opening happens, not everything will be completely harmonious. Of course not. You all have free will and different agendas and will always have that. What we are saying is that the current change underway has always been the plan. Now newer, lighter, less dense energies have come in with more and more embodiments. More and more humans have been bringing in this new vibration, and in reaction, the resistance has been quite intense and is escalating. Yet, the ascension into a higher dimension of possibility for growth is underway. You are part of this phase of growth for humanity and the Earth.

A new plane of energies

When we use the word ascension we are speaking in the language of your third-dimensional reality where things exist in linear and hierarchical concepts. We could say that the Earth and humanity are making a transition to a different plane of energies. It is neither higher nor lower. It is different. The difference is in the nature of the vibrations that are the most easily supported. The movement is to higher vibrations than those typical of a three-dimensional plane. By higher, we mean less dense, holding more light, vibrating at a higher frequency.

Think of your eyes having blinders on. In a three-dimensional world you grew up with fairly thick blinders, but over time perhaps you began to remove some of the density and were able to see, understand, take in more light. On a higher dimensional plane, on the plane to which humanity and the Earth are transitioning, humans will be born with blinders that are much less dense, so that they will have a greater ability to see, know, and feel connection to others, to feel and express with support, love, kindness and compassion.

There will always be those who struggle with darker, denser blinders, but the majority of humans will come in less fettered by the conditions and experiences of those lower, denser vibrations. So when we use the term ascension we are talking about a transition, but it is also right to think about this as an evolutionary change.

Why is it that the history of humanity is about war, greed, territory, war, hate? We are talking about the evolution of humanity to a state of being where those elements of history do not need to be repeated because there will be new understandings, new values, new approaches to living, to connecting with others, with the Earth, with the Divine.

In this new state of being, humans will grow into knowing and feeling the sense of connection to Divine Source creation energies. We are not saying that you will no longer have machines or technologies, we are saying you will move in different directions because the values driving the creation and inventions and work will be different.

We will continue to use the words love, kindness, connection and compassion because the energy of those words touches an important part of you. It encourages you to call those energies forward and reminds you that you own the power of those qualities.

You are in the midst of an ascension, transition, evolution. This is where the Earth is going. This is where humanity is going. There has always been the potential for this transition to be made but the shift requires a buildup of light among the human population. You have seen spiritual gurus and teachers as the bringers of light, and many are. But it is the masses of people who are holding hope for humanity, through their love for the Earth, love for their fellow humans, kindness for the store clerk, compassion for the young mother and the homeless man on the corner. Those who in their everyday lives are listening to their hearts. All these light holders are part of what is making the transition possible. It is underway. It is happening.

Look at the youth and what they believe, what they support and what they reject. Young people brought about ecological activism on a larger scale. Young people pushed caring for endangered species. We do not mean to say that older, wise and loving humans weren't always present to these concerns, but the sheer numbers of young voices added great weight. Look at your social issues and environmental issues and you will see the numbers and trends of young people who are advancing the light surrounding the Earth and emanating from humanity.

The Earth and humanity need your hope for the future. The Earth and humanity need your heart. Nothing is born to remain unchanging. The Earth was born as a planet and evolves every day. But the Earth's evolution is linked to that of humanity. The Earth cannot progress in its expression of creation unless humanity moves forward as well.

Humans have always been evolving, but the evolution has had constraints based on the core energies of a third-dimensional planet in which everything is separated, disconnected, divided, categorized, placed into hierarchies. As more humans began to reject these as the limited givens of their existence and expression, then the energies soaking into the Earth's field slowly began to change.

There are now sufficient lighter vibrations to allow the Earth to move. As part of that change, the Earth will heal itself. You are seeing the effects of all the damage that has been done to the Earth but we want to encourage you to see it as the healing that is part of the Earth's evolution.

Understanding ascension

To imagine ascending, let us take a mountain as the example. You go up the mountain and there are changes in the air. It becomes thinner. It feels different in your body and your body reacts differently to it. As you ascend the mountain there are also changes in what grows. The vegetation and the fauna may change as you reach different altitudes. And as you ascend, what you can see when you gaze outward also changes. The higher you go, the more you can see.

Consider that you currently live at sea level and that the only mountains you have are no more than hills. You take walks at sea level. You take a path that goes up a hill, but you never get high enough to see past the other hills in your area. Your sight is limited. The air quality is depressed as if there were a ceiling holding all the particles and pollution within a sphere.

You see our point. There are many advantages to ascending. And the ascension we speak of is not a visit. The whole of the planet moves into that plane of lighter air, greater clarity and breadth of vision. And with that comes greater understanding. There is less in the way. What surrounds you is different because it is supported by the vibrations of this altitude.

We do not need to overwork this metaphor. Who would not wish to see life and the world from the vantage point of a beautiful mountaintop? Imagine that on this mountain top there are seas and forests and all that beauty that the Earth is able to create, without the history of damage and wounding caused by those confined to the lower altitudes of third-dimensional thinking and seeing and acting.

Unlike journeys to the tops of mountains, your ascension requires only that you open your heart, that you choose to open to love, compassion and kindness; to receiving it and to sending it forth into the world. As you do this, the light of your being expands and shines forth and those vibrations that you are sending forth lead you and your fellow humans upward to a higher vibrational dimension.

Remember that though we use the word higher in your language, we do not think in terms of hierarchies. There are differences in the predominate vibrations. Some are denser and some are lighter. You are moving from denser vibrations and the forms that those vibrations support, to lighter vibrations and the forms of being that those lighter vibrations support.

For the Earth, Source creation energies will unfold with greater lightness of touch. The wisdom of the Earth's elements will be more easily available to humans and there will be the possibility of more active learning from the Earth about how to create, how to make exchanges of energies and even the notion of transmutation applied, with the Earth's blessing, to creating with its resources.

With the ascension to a higher vibrational base for life there will be those who try to remain bound to denser energies. There are many soul lessons still to be learned by some that relate to the third-dimensional plane, but these learners will not be disruptors of the higher vibrational plane. Instead, their lessons will be more easily accomplished because of the models that the fifth-dimensional plane affords.

We want to give you an experience of the higher vibrational plane to which the Earth and humanity will be moving.

Meditation on ascension

Place your body in a comfortable position. Take a few deep breaths and allow your body to settle. Soften into quietness. Ask those in spirit who are present to support you in opening and expanding your heart. Set an intention of opening your subtle awareness to the energies beyond your skin.

Let the words and activities of your day subside. Let your awareness and your breath now focus on your first chakra.

As you breathe into your first chakra, feel the breath expand the chakra. With each breath expand further until you feel the energy of your first chakra outside your skin merging with that closest layer of your etheric energies. Rest here a moment in this slight expansion of your awareness.

Continue this with each chakra, each time allowing the breath to help open the chakra energies and allowing the chakra energies to flow outward into your etheric bodies and auric field.

As you bring your awareness to the seventh chakra at the crown, allow the sensation of the whole of you breathing as one thing—the whole body, the whole field nourished by the Breath.

Now, with each breath allow even greater expansion, where there is no boundary, just joy and a sense of the greater whole. There is the possibility of knowing Oneness. Light surrounds you. The light is you.

This state of Being becomes a natural part of a life that is fully supported on a plane of higher vibrations.

You are a Being who can help bring this about. You are a midwife to the evolution of your species and the entire planet. Hold this knowing.

When you are ready, bring your awareness back to your physical body, aware of your muscles and how you sit or lie. You can always return, but now intend to be fully in your physical form.[5]

You are a pioneer

We are going to continue speaking with you about the meaning of the ascension of the Earth and humanity. It is difficult for you to grasp how the changes will come about even as you may attempt to imagine what life for humans would be like if there were no dense darker forces wreaking destruction everywhere on your planet in every system—human, environmental, ecological, social, economic. You can

---

5   This guided meditation is also available in audio format on Spiritwoven.com.

look anywhere and see how the current patterns of behavior, which are also the historical patterns, are destructive to morale and growth. So with all this destructive energy, which appears so embedded in your world, no matter the culture, how will evolving to a higher level of being happen?

When you see the escalation of greed, hate, war, you see the world as an increasingly hostile place for the majority of people. What we see is the reaction to the threat of change. The light in you, the light in millions upon millions of human beings, is threatening the way of living and believing that has taken root on the Earth. Your light and the light of others is uprooting the assurance that the old assumptions will prevail. Look for the changes. Look at the young people. Attitudes that are more generous, more accepting, more open are showing up in very young people. They are coming into this world with a greater attunement to higher vibrations. You are a pioneer. There are waves of settlers who will come into maturity as the ascension energies increase. You are paving the way. Your light is pushing against the denser vibrations.

You are experiencing the process of new creation. When you create something new, materials, ideas, expectations are being destroyed, by which we mean changed. When it comes to humans, change is often resisted and so when you bring light to darkness, many of those who have found their sense of self and made their way in the darkness rebel, looking for ways to ensure the continuation of the darkness they have known. In the past, when more light was introduced, the vibrations of humanity and the planet provided more support for those seeking to dim the light, to turn it away. But now there is enough light so that although there is the escalating reaction, it will not succeed. It will be painful. Many will leave the planet because some clearing is necessary for the new to grow. Those who leave the planet will take all their lessons home to their soul to enrich the learning. All experience is valuable. But we are not here to speak on that subject. We are here to speak with you about being a pioneer.

If you have read about the early pioneers on your planet, you know that it was not easy. There were no roads, there were no stores, there were no conveniences. What existed was the drive to go forward, to explore, to learn as much as possible and to share that knowledge. Just so, you as a pioneer in helping to bring the Earth and humanity to a new reality will not look around and see signposts for fifth-dimension stores. There are some signs, like this book for example, but you must have the intention to find them. You must have curiosity and dedication. You must have hope and an open heart and then you must ask for guidance and support. Resistance and suspicion are part of your human, third-dimensional processes. And yet an open heart will always guide you truly in the most important things.

Pioneers must be strong. You do not have to cut down trees to make a path, you do not have to train to be an astronaut to explore the moon or distant planets, but you do need to train your heart to stay open and your hope to stay alive in the face of injustice, hatred, corruption, greed, the decimation of cities and cultures, and environmental catastrophes. There will be events continuing that are overwhelming in their depravity and destruction.

As a pioneer you must be able to avoid getting lost in despair, sadness, anger. As a pioneer you must think, feel and act from love, not react in the pattern of lower third-dimensional vibrations. We are not saying that you should ignore what is occurring. We are saying that it is important for you to focus on where the planet is going, where humanity is going—away from greed, hate, and injustice, toward a foundation of love, kindness, compassion, generosity; toward creation that springs from love, kindness and compassion, not from greed and disrespect for the humanity of others; toward creation that comes out of the awareness of the connection of all that is.

How would a world look where those were the foundations? That is the world you are pioneering. For you it is a dream. The pioneers at every century in all time have held a dream, believed in a dream and taken the early steps into the potential held in their heart, in their imagination. We are here to tell you that this is not an ephemeral dream. The ascension is a reality that is already underway. There are many pioneers. The next important stage is the joining together of all these lanterns helping to lead the way.

The Earth and humanity are partners

We are going to discuss the reason that planets go through their own evolutionary process. Planets, like people, have creation energy, that is, they have the ability to create. The creation energy within a soul provides the ability to create, to experiment and to learn and grow. As each soul learns and expands, its ability to use its creation energy increases. Each time a soul invests its purposes and creation energy in an embodiment, it is in the service of its growth, its expansion of light.

A planet is born and comes into being with a large amount of creation energy and a process of evolving. It experiments with the raw elements to which it has access and as it is assembling its materials, new opportunities are created. It is not separate from the universe in which it grows. It is part of the universe in which it is growing. It is energetically connected to the stars and planets that surround it.

You think people are separate in their individuality but in truth all souls and the embodiments that souls create are connected. This is the hardest concept for you to understand as you seek to open to greater knowledge of the reality of the oneness of all.

As the Earth formed with its connection to the larger planetary and star systems, creation energies also embedded planetary purposes. A central purpose of Earth is to be a place for souls to grow and learn with. It takes time to grow a planet, and as the Earth grew there were gifts that were brought to her. The magnetic fields were organized and certain other shaping elements were brought into being. There are those beings who oversee the shaping of different aspects of a planet's creation. The creation of a planet is a great undertaking, and many very ancient beings and energies are present to assist in the formative moments to ensure that there will be possibilities for the intended purposes to be achieved.

As the Earth grew, it was seeded with energies from other beings who came to create and to experiment and to bring their own genetic material to the life that was forming and the beings who would come. The Earth was not alone in its development. As the Earth energies settled, more and more different ones came to bring their DNA and to seed their knowledge to further prepare the Earth for the development of the human species. You count the age of being from your own limited knowledge of the Earth and the universe, but where we are there is no time, there is only the joy of creation. And creation always means change.

The Earth's mission has always been to become a place supporting the growth of souls. And it was known that there was the potential of a new species for embodiment. That species, the human species, would be connected to the Earth, interacting with the Earth's energies, entwined with the Earth in evolving.

So it is that the Earth and humanity are in a joint partnership, a joint enterprise to expand in consciousness and in connection to the oneness of all. It is a long road. As a human you must first come to know yourself as a whole and a whole connected to others and connected to the planet. Harm to one is harm to all. That is what we would like to emphasize: harm to one is harm to all. When the Earth is harmed, you are harmed, and every human, every living thing is harmed.

The joint mission of the Earth and humanity is to move from what you call a third-dimensional plane of existence to a higher plane where the ability to know connection is much stronger and much more supported; where knowing that harm to the Earth or harm to another is felt and held energetically by all.

The energies of harm need to be transmuted, not just cleared. They need to be transmuted into healing energies that flow back through all the web of connection. It is not complicated. It merely requires concentration and intent at a deep level.

A more conscious partnership with Earth

So today we will talk more about the planet. When humans open to higher vibrations, those new vibrations manifest in what is expressed and in what those humans create with their energies. Their expression resonates in other humans. The vibrations carried in expression of these higher energies become part of the air that others breathe in through their own energy fields. Physical manifestations in the form of ideas and objects come forth that are more in alignment with the higher vibrations, particularly those of connection and inclusion. That is, as humans hold higher vibrations, their creations and their problem-solving innovations move outward through the vibrations that hold awareness of connection and the mission of service to the greater whole. The greater good, as you say, is paramount in this use of the creation energies.

The Earth's creation energies were focused initially on emergence, of coming into being in physical manifestation. Once initiated, many processes of emergence became automatic; there were forces set in motion and those continued their movement, their growth and expression for eons. The Earth was also created to allow for human embodiment and soul learning. And so the early energies of the Earth were aligned with early human attempts to come into realization as beings. As the Earth continued to grow, now with the presence of humans, interaction increased. Humans found the Earth to be bountiful in opportunities for nourishment, for shelter, for wonder. As the human populations spread, the connections with the Earth as a resource were developed in many different ways. The nature of the Earth in different parts of the world led to different relations, different experiences of the Earth as a home. Humans were very adaptable and the Earth, in its interactions with humans, was in balance for millennia as you count time.

But as human populations grew and structures became more elaborate, the connection between the Earth and humans became muddied and greater amounts of disconnection occurred, until the stance valued by many was 'the human against the Earth.' The conquering of the Earth by humans has led to many disruptions of the Earth's creation energies.

The Earth's development and growth has always sought to support human embodiments, to support soul learning. As humans develop, the Earth changes and grows to support the learning opportunities of souls. But the Earth was never meant to be a place of complete disconnection. The robbing, destroying, and diminishing of its bounty and creations—not for the good of all, but for the benefit of the few—has been damaging to the Earth's own evolutionary progress, linked with the assumed progress of humanity.

Now, as more and more humans feel the need for change and connection with the greater whole; the drive toward very different solutions to the world's desperate problems; the need to create *with* the Earth and not in opposition to it—as all this grows, those energies join with the Earth's own higher energies, impulses and mission as a planet.

As the Earth is able to call forth and receive higher vibrations, the Earth's creation energies are amplified. There is much Earth activity now, and this will continue in the coming years because those energies are once again being fed and nourished. The Earth has damage to heal and new creations to put forward that will serve the future humans who will again work in partnership with the Earth. Realizing that the Earth is a partner, not an enemy to human well-being, will engender new ways of working with all the Earth's resources.

Like humans, the Earth has a field of energies. Those energies have been veiled by the denser vibrations that humans amplified. But as the planet receives higher vibrational expressions from more and more humans, the joint enterprise of ascending to a higher vibrational plane advances. The creation energies that flow from the Earth will meet and partner with the energies of humans who themselves are emitting and evoking and connecting with higher vibrations.

The Earth will look much the same, with waters and different Earth-made formations, but there will be topographical shifts and changes of weather patterns and earth movements; conditions will change as the Earth seeks health and balance. Those changes, when embraced and accepted as part of the process, will be the start of a new partnership between humans and the Earth. Both will benefit. The Earth seeks harmony in its creations and in its support for the embodiments for whom it is a temporary home, partner and teacher.

Humans seek the nourishment that their Mother Earth can provide. What a different relationship this will become.

The Earth's changes

As part of the ascension process, the Earth will undergo changes at many levels. While the core of the planet will remain much as it is, the energies, by which we mean the electrical magnetic resonances that are emanating from the core, will be shifting. The changes occur from the outside in and from the inside outward. There is always a flow. When there are changes at any level, there are impacts through the entire Earth. It is the same for humans on the Earth. When outer experiences enter the field of the human, they flow through and into the body and then back out into the larger field. All is connected even when the effects are imperceptible to human senses or awarenesses.

Regarding the planet, as the energies of the outer field increase, these higher vibrations move down into the Earth. In the layers of the Earth where so much of the dense energies reside, it is difficult for the higher vibrations to accumulate or flow. Yet there are places on Earth where there is deeper penetration of the higher vibrations and the connection to the Earth has been maintained. As those vibrations move more deeply into the Earth, they spread out and bring a new energy that supports the Earth's healing and the Earth's ability to adjust to a higher vibration. This has been happening for some time.

As those energies move more deeply inward there are resonances that move back up toward the denser layers of the Earth where there has been damage to the creation energies that inhabit every part of the Earth. All that has been and will be created by the Earth is alive with creation energies. But you can understand that to heal the damage done to the Earth's surfaces and creations requires a significant amount of energy.

This means that there will be disruptions to all the Earth's manifestations, particularly in those areas where there is the least connection to knowing and loving the Earth. All that you fear in terms of earthquakes, tidal waves, storms, volcanic eruptions, droughts and fires will cause humanity to move away from the affected areas and toward increased care of the Earth. These are part of the changes that will allow the ascension of the Earth and the ascension of humanity.

The internal energies of the Earth will begin to return to patterns aligned with its purpose of ascension as the higher vibration energies increase, driven in part by changes in humanity's vibrational balances, as well as new frequencies from the larger field in which the planet exists. You know that the magnetic field changes, but other underlying energetic patterns affecting the planet's expression also change. These patterns were part of the Earth's formation, stemming from its Divine purpose of manifesting different levels of creation, through the higher vibrations and interventions to assist in the long-range development of the Earth and the human species. From the perspective of nonlinear time, all that was occurring was just an event in the energetic reality. When all is connected, the harmonious flow of light and potential exists in an endless sphere of being. It is too much even for us to fully comprehend, so all we can do is point you to the far horizon of what you might one day come to approach more closely, as we do in our own being.

The Earth is on its own course of possibilities and potentials but as we have said, the Earth's path and that of the human being are joined. Souls learn through their embodiments. Earth is a place where many souls incarnate to learn and grow. The Earth needs the cooperation and partnership of the ensouled humans embodying on its surface in order to move into own fuller potential.

Partnerships are strong when there is an understanding of mutual benefit and future, when there is a deeply loving connection that is embraced and cherished. When you cherish the Earth, you are cherishing your own potential and fullness of being.

The purpose of this book is to provide you with some ways of knowing, thinking and responding during this transition stage of the ascension process, so that you may strengthen your own being while supporting that which the Earth must express as part of opening to a higher state of being.

You are on Earth to learn

The pandemic you experienced brought indications of what is to come. The presence of the virus, continuing its mutations and forms and spreading, seeded ideas that the future will be different from what has been. Living with pressures from unseen elements that bring disease, pain, and death has long been present. But the pandemic and its aftermath has brought new levels of uncertainty, suspicion and fear, which are now well-seeded. During the pandemic there was the sense that this particular virus would arise and be very difficult, bringing much death, pain and fear, but then there would be a solution and life would return to normal. This has not and will not be the case. There will continue to be ever-present threats, as you see them, to physical health; there will continue to be larger losses of life. The idea of security will be challenged in the years to come.

In a time of increased vulnerability, where is the place to be? Your home is not on the Earth. Your home is with soul. Your home is with spirit. So when you are on the Earth plane your task is not to feel at home, but to feel that you are learning through experiences of the pleasant kind and the unpleasant kind, as you categorize such things. But you are not at home. You are away at school to learn. And when you are away at school you have many vulnerabilities. You are with strangers. You are with people who are very different. You are uncertain where you belong.

Your greatest potential for comfort is in remembering that this is not home. Remember that you are here as a student. Remember that your primary connection is with your soul and your soul's purposes for which you are the student. You are here to experience and to learn from what you experience so that the light and richness of your soul—of which you are an aspect—may expand. When you remember your home, there is nothing to fear. What is painful is learned from. What is joyful is learned from. What is puzzling is a path for learning. You, as your soul's representative, can learn from all the emotions and states of being you experience. Choose to experience what you are experiencing fully; do not turn away—embrace it.

We want to reinforce the notion that now is the time for you to connect ever more deeply with your sense of your spirit home, your sense of you as a Being of spirit, who is temporarily in form on this plane as part of your soul's growth and expansion. You are here on this plane at this time to be one who can help to expand the light that surrounds and benefits the planet, and to aid others in connecting with their true essence. It is a big task. It is not an easy task. You have been away for a long time. And so, remember, remember, remember. That is where comfort will be most strongly available to you.

Love and joy are your birthright

When you come onto this planet, onto this plane, there is so much for you that is yours by right. You understand that teaching, wisdom and great love flows to you from the Earth, just as Divine creation energy flows down to you through your soul. Which means that though you may sometimes feel that you must search for love, look for hope, wait for joy, we want to remind you that love is your birthright. It is there for you.

It is not difficult to find when you go inside yourself; when you feel deeply into the Earth and let Gaia's energy flow up to you. When you are in your heart and rest there, you rest in a place that holds the love of the universe for you. It is never far away from you. It does not have to be searched for. Among all the swirl of this plane, amid all the distress and disappointment and betrayals and disruptions, within you abides this wellspring of love in its purest form. There are no conditions. It is yours and it only waits to be claimed.

We want to remind you that just as love is your birthright, so too is joy. Many seek big experiences to have joy, but each of you has the ability to find joy in the smallest of things. In the smallest of moments, you can experience the joy of beauty, of being, of lightness. It can come in a small growing thing. It can come in a sound. It can come from any aspect that is around you. Where you put your attention and allow, joy is waiting for you.

In this time of so much sadness, so much destruction, it is important for you to know that it is not yours to be caught up in that. It is yours to own who you are in your own Beingness; to own what has been given to you for you to delight in. We understand that it is very difficult amid everything that is going on outside, and what you may be holding from reactions to your personal life experiences. But allow yourself to come into the home of *you*. Come into the deep truth of yourself, for in that truth is your connection to Divine love, to your soul, to joy, peace and freedom.

Yes, it is strange that amid so much constraint, we are saying there is freedom for you when you go into your Being. Go into the truth of your Being; not what is shown to you, not what is told to you, not what you see reflected by others, not the stories you tell yourself. When you are in You, in that place there is such richness and lightness. What the Earth needs, what all beings need, is for that birthright of joy and love and lightness to blossom, to be claimed, to be allowed and to be set free. Let it flow from you.

Each moment that you are in that place of deep connection with the truth of your Being, those energies flow out from you. Even if you are not speaking, they flow out from you and they take their place in the field of the planet. As more of you allow those moments, there is a greater field of lightness and love and joy that can bring some balance, and a better future for all.

Address your fears

When you consider what is happening on the Earth right now, you are often very concerned about the changes in the weather patterns, change to the air, the waters, the forests, the kingdoms of living things. Your news is filled with warnings and distressing news of loss. It is true that unexpected events, variations, changes, forms arising and fading are all part of what occurs in nature's organic flow. But you know that many of the changes you are seeing are the result of interventions and abuses of the Earth's lifegiving resources. A gift of living on the Earth is the opportunity to invent and to create with great freedom. When that freedom is exercised without being anchored in the long-term well-being of the human community, as well as other living things and the planet as an integrated whole, then there are consequences on many levels.

When you see the consequences, fear arises: fear of loss, fear of change, fear of danger, fear of the impossibility of sustaining life, your own and others. When fear arises, nothing improves, and nothing positive results. Fear is a destroyer of many things. It is an incredibly powerful force. And yet you unleash your fears constantly on yourself and on others. You unleash them in your communities and worldwide. And not only the fear that is expressed, but also unexpressed fear that you feel can move out from you and add to others' fears, which are already present in the environment.

We would say, 'Do you wish to live in an environment that is filled with fear?' If you do not, then the first step begins with you. Every step begins with a single individual. What can you do? What is within your power?

You can address your own fear.

We know that it is difficult to accept that finding the seeds of fear in yourself is the first step toward contributing to the betterment of your family, your community and the planet as a whole. But some part of you knows that you are not just one individual, you are part of a larger whole. And only in facing your fears can you stop nourishing them and begin to remove them.

We do not mean to suggest that this is simple. It takes a strong intention and a willingness to explore deeply within to find and understand the old roots of fears; to find those that arose from within as a protection and those that were absorbed unconsciously from others.

When fear is removed, love can flow. You can choose to bring forth the love that is yours to summon. You all have a greater capacity to love than you currently know. Your ability to love is innate, a part of your very essence. That love is what you need to be cultivating and harvesting for your own benefit and the benefit of all living things; for the benefit of the Earth.

Part of love is acceptance. Part of love is not knowing or expecting an outcome from something you desire. Love is a way of Being. So what you can do today and in all your days is to call forth from within you the love that you have the right and the ability to generate, to express, to let flow from you. That is our wish for you. That is the world we wish for you.

Know the love you carry

We wish to continue talking about the nature of the ascension energies and what that means with respect to the changes on the Earth.

Many of you have experienced places that you found creepy or that felt unsafe, even in daylight. Sometimes there were visual signals of concern. Sometimes there was something that looked normal but did not feel okay to your senses. You were feeling energies, yes? During the time when there was experimenting with hallucinogenic drugs there was the phrase 'good vibrations' and now there is talk of 'bad vibes.' There is reality to those energies that feel good, safe, welcoming and those that don't. When you walk into a room of people, how does the room feel? You have had different experiences of this even if you have not talked about it this way. You had a feeling before anything welcoming or unwelcoming was said or done. Perhaps there is energy in the room carrying over from something sad or joyous that preceded the current gathering. Perhaps many of the people in the room are carrying anger or sadness or contentment and their individual energies are creating the vibration you feel. You are feeling the accumulated energies.

Just so there are certain vibrations—energies—that have been present on the Earth for eons. Over many thousands of years, higher vibrations were introduced and woven into the Earth's basic template, the energetic template. Those higher vibrations came from many different outside sources. The Earth's own creation energies have manifested primarily through the creations of the elements. As humanity's presence grew on the surface, the vibrations and energies and actions that humans put forth became part of the Earth's creation experience.

Clearly, some of these vibrations have been beneficial and some destructive. If you thought of the Earth as a Being, then when you interacted with it you would act out of respect for this enormous expression of creation energy. Indeed, there have been many cultures where interactions with the Earth were based on profound respect and love. There were also those cultures where the interactions of respect were based on fear. Which vibrations do you think benefitted the Earth and humanity more?

All of this is to say that the Earth is changing to become a place where the vibrations most easily supported and experienced will be those of love and kindness. There will always be some who hold on to fear because they, as their soul's representative, are still working on how to hold love and not let fear take root. But just as some soils are better for growing some things rather than others, the Earth will become a place where love grows, where the nourishment for love is high. It will not be a soil conducive to hate. Humans on this Earth will have less and less acceptance of hate, while at the same time seeing as worthy of compassion and help those in whom fear has taken root and hatred has arisen. Can you even imagine such a world? And yet this is the future toward which humanity and the Earth are moving.

You will still have to shelter and feed everyone. You will still want to keep everyone as healthy as their body and purpose deems right. You will still need to grow food, have transportation, figure out how to have clean water everywhere and find room in your hearts for everyone. This is not the picture of what will be in place next year or even in 50 years, though there will be progress visible even 10 years from now. The balance of the vibrations has already shifted a small bit and that has triggered the massive reactions and escalation of fear and violence. What you see as rising is actually falling. That is the first thing to remember. It is not just one empire that is falling, it is all of them. This is not a change that is localized to your community, your country. It is worldwide.

Our purpose here is to help you see that you are winning. The higher vibrations are on course to predominate. Love is already the strongest vibration. You cannot see in your media the presence of escalating love, but it is there underneath the sorrow, within the compassion, held high by those who choose to hold on to their hope for the future, to express love despite the tumultuous cacophony of pain and anger, hate and injustice. Humanity as a whole has reached a point in its development where a new future state of being is evolving.

This transition state that you find yourself living in is difficult. Within you, you have recourse to anger, hate, sadness, and depression that can block your own higher states of being. You are in your essence a being of light and a being with a deep reservoir of unconditional love. Your task is to know the supplies you carry with you on this pioneering journey; to know that you have access to a deep reservoir for replenishment, which means you can spend your love, compassion and kindness wildly, without fear. You can glory in your ability to open to Love, to open to compassion and to open to unlimited kindness, because you have, and will continue to have, more and more of it.

We offer our words in this book to encourage you to find the joy in being a pioneer of the high heart as you make this journey of helping the Earth and humanity reach their new ascended template for being.

A great task is before you

We recommend that you view the film *The Year the Earth Changed* because what it brings forward is an experience of the breath of the Earth.

There was much that was difficult during the pandemic that circled the globe. Humans were forced into isolation, into their own contained limited space. There was much suffering in trying to live within these pressed-in boundaries, these constraints of space and movement.

And yet there were good things that arose. Humans are very creative, and so there were many forms of adaptation—for example, using screens to see each other and speak with each other and do business. There were some positive aspects to the pandemic. You were not in your cars, in traffic.

But it was stressful at the same time. There you were, locked in place either alone or with others. Some of you sat in your cars or in a closet for privacy. In your normal pre-pandemic times, you moved about. You had more choice, more richness of environments that you could move yourself to outside of your homes and your rooms.

The cost to you was of benefit to the Earth. During the pandemic cars stopped moving, people stopped moving.

Air and shipping traffic was reduced. And what happened? Earth was quiet. There was peace. And on your screens, you saw amazing pictures of animals moving into city landscapes, moving into towns, villages and resorts. Not only was there more freedom of movement for animals that had been pressed into ever smaller environments for their survival, but also the Earth was able to breathe more freely when released from the commotion in the air, on the ground, and in the waters. In the silence of that space, the Earth could breathe. The birds, animals, fish, plants, trees—they breathed more deeply, and life flourished in that breath. Yes, life flourished. But it should not be that the humans must be locked inside, for all to have breath, to have space, to have health.

Is there not a way forward where all are healthy? Yes, there will always be illnesses and problems, but those can be easily resolved when the environment as a whole is healthy. The magic of the creation energies, which each of you hold within you, will allow you, if you choose, to find the pathway so that humans can be out—not confined, but out in their environment—and yet still the other parts of Earth can breathe and be healthy. This is the great task before you.

It is clear that healing the Earth in all its aspects— human, animal, plant, water, air, soil cannot be accomplished without the addition of an infusion of new energies. But you can begin to participate in that healing process. You must choose to care about the whole. Know you are not alone. Know that you are seen and that there is support for you. Understand that you must first care for yourself as part of the whole.

If you can increase your connection to the whole, then as the whole becomes healthier and moves energetically to a higher plane, you too move forward. You too ascend into a state of grace—a state of greater health, of greater love, of greater happiness, of greater ease—because you are aligned with health for all, with wholeness.

Expand the peace within you

For those of you who have awakened in this time of possibility, this time of the shifting of the vibration of the planet and therefore the potential shifting of the vibrations into which there may be human embodiments, your goal must now be to not only stay awake but to find that place of peace within you that you can expand. Energies around you will shift and become increasingly chaotic, potentially violent, with increasing anger, distress, sadness and worry. All these energies will be swirling.

Creating within you that place of peacefulness does not mean you are disregarding events. You have compassion. You want to assist in helping others. But first you must create that place within you that is a place of peacefulness that is always there for you to go to. You cannot calm others if you are not first in a calm place. We understand it is very difficult not to be distressed when you see distress; not to empathetically feel the pain or sadness of others. But this is not what is helpful.

The place of true empathy comes from a place of deep calm. It is not that you are isolated from or unaware of others' suffering or anger. It is that you sit in a place of deep peace, from which you can put forward kindness, compassion, love, assistance. You may not know what is the correct assistance to provide to another. You will use your abilities—your empathic, intuitive, psychic abilities, your spiritual connections—to try to understand what will benefit and not bring harm to another. But you can only know what you are allowed to know.

Sometimes the course that an individual must follow for their own purposes—seemingly misaligned with their soul purposes—is what they must experience. It is part of their path. Your goal is not to remove people from the path they are on. You might assist them by helping them better understand the path they're on or seeing that there might be options or choices. But you cannot truly know what is right for them. This does not mean you do not seek to help. You offer healing. You offer love. You offer your hand. That is what you do from a place of calm.

When you are in a place of calm, that energy radiates out. It helps. If all of you who are awakened to the current possibilities continually seek to express from that place of deep calm, that place of deep peace will be soothing to others. Calm is very soothing in the face of disruption. In the face of what you will call emergencies, calm is what is called for.

There will be many emergencies, as you call them—many emergencies that will need calm. Whether you are distant or close, your energetic calm is beneficial, soothing. So that is what we want you to hold. Find that place of calm within you. Seek to expand it. Make it a place within you that you know how to get to—the frequently trodden path, the well-worn path. Make calm a destination within you that you are visiting, sitting in, resting in and appreciating. As it benefits you, it will benefit others, even those at a distance, unknown to you.

Find stillness

There are energies that have accumulated that are not beneficial and there are energies that are present that can be activated more fully to balance what is not beneficial and move the balance toward that which will be of greater benefit and health for the planet and for all that lives and exists on the planet. Nurturing those beneficial energies in your own being is one important step.

If you were able to slow your sensations by slowing the input—closing the eyes, blocking the ears, lessening awareness through the skin—what would result? When there is no light or sound, there is a sense of deep stillness. And when you have that sense of deep stillness, you do not feel fear or other emotions, you are just being. That is one way to think about the senses being quieted so that you can feel yourself expand, so that you can sense the larger you beyond the skin. It is beneficial for everyone to find stillness—enough stillness so that they can feel their own being, outside of the input from others.

For those who want to be more deeply connected with their own essence and deeply connected to the Earth, the idea of the You that does not stop at the skin resonates. This is the You aware of a field of energy, a sphere of surrounding energy. And we are not talking about the energies of those who come to help, but about energies from the soul, from the essence of Being.

That essence is not limited to the size of the body. It is not about having a big personality. There are people you call charismatic and you think it is because of their personality. But indeed, it is the energy that they radiate, the energies that surround them. This is why you can walk into a room and there are people that you are drawn to. Now, perhaps your senses have something to do with it—you are attracted to them because you consider them handsome or beautiful or you are drawn to the sound of their melodious or resonant voice. But sometimes you are drawn by what you would call their energy.

It would be interesting, would it not, if you walked into a room with your eyes closed and your ears blocked, and all you had was a sensation of knowing that you could come to no harm. As if there were those who would gently keep you safe. Where would you be drawn to moving and what would cause you to move in that way? And now let's give you an intention. 'I wish to move in the direction of energies that would feel good to me. I wish the essence of my being, the energies of my being to guide me to the energies of another with whom there would be a compatible, complementary connection.' And then you allow yourself to just trust that in asking such a thing, it could happen.

What we are saying is that to be able to heal yourself, and to help heal others and the planet, you must first be aware of your own fuller being. There are many ways to do this. First, find the part of you that yearns to know your fuller, deeper self. We are not talking about emotional analysis, though emotional pain and emotional pleasures are all part of the layers that have to do with living on this planet. But underneath all of that is the expression of your own deeper essence. And so that becomes a first step, to find within your own being the desire to truly know yourself. Not to work on your personality, not to fix what you might consider your personality flaws, not even to bask in what you enjoy most about your personality, but to come to know your true essence.

Think of personality as what you get dressed in every day. What is underneath that? You get dressed every day, you wear your clothes and underneath that is your body. Inside your skin are your organs, all that makes the physical body. We are not talking about that. You have an array of emotions, a variety of thoughts. You make decisions, you have experiences. We are not talking about that.

Beyond all that is a deeper knowing, and a first step is to connect with the desire to know the deeper self that holds the essence of your being. From that place of what we could call the soul of the self, much knowing opens. Wisdom opens, healing opens, helping others in the deepest, most profound way opens.

Feed the light

There is much distress because of the wars that are occurring now. As wars and conflicts arise, we want to remind everyone that you are helping every time you do your own work of clearing and raising your own vibration—through prayer, through meditation, by connecting with those in spirit. Every time you tune in to your intention to contribute to healing the planet and all living things, every time you embrace joy, allowing joy to light up your own soul, your own energy field, you are helping because this energy moves out from you.

It is not just prayers that move out from you. Your energies move out from you when you intend to move to a higher vibration, to bring in the light. When you seek to bring in the light and to expand the light in you, it goes out from you, and that accumulating light is a balance for the darkness that war and death and fear and anger create. So as much as the lower self wants to talk and think about punishment and revenge—all of the anger put into words, even if not put into action—every time that happens it further depresses the energy surrounding the planet, and it feeds those lower energies.

We want to remind you to be one who feeds the light. Your intention to expand the light within you and to expand the light surrounding the world, to raise your own vibration to an expanded higher state—every time you do this, you help your entire planet, your entire plane of existence. You feed to the world the light that is so much needed.

Our focus is on the rising energies supporting the ascension of humankind to an expanded awareness and consciousness, but we know that there will be darkness. There will be this disruption and turmoil. Your work is to not feed that, but instead to focus on the light, on the higher vibrations of love and the intention of expansion, of oneness, of harmony, even in the midst of conflict. This is not easy to do. The lower self feels upset, angry, sad and wants to respond. That is very understandable, and when you have those feelings, immediately note them and honor your response to the energies you are seeing. And then choose to move to provide balance, moving the scale in the direction of the higher vibration, in the direction of the light.

This is an honorable task. It is the work of warriors—warriors of the light who act not out of anger or grief or sadness, but out of love. You are a warrior of love. Not of the lower order that the word 'warrior' evokes, but as one who, despite all that is occurring, holds to the higher heart-centered order of love, which is free from agendas, free from self-interest, free from ego. It is a love that seeks the benefit of all. That is power.

We offer these words because this is a time of very intense suffering, not just in the places of active war and aggression, but everywhere. The places of war serve as focal points for bringing forward all the accumulated grief and upset and worry and anger from all of that has gone awry, all that is in pain, wounded, suffering. And that feeds more of the darkness.

So it is a cycle, you see, and your role—which you have already chosen, whether you are conscious of it or not—is to be on the side of increasing the light, increasing the love. You are needed now. And there are many, many by your side—those of us who are not in bodies, all the archangels and the angels and the master teachers and the teachers and the guides and the helpers—all of us are with you, supporting you. None of you are alone. All of you have help. Call on that help. Ask for support as you seek to expand the light and the love that you send out into the world.

Look to your heart for meaning

Holidays that are broadly shared are times of great potential for opening to love, joy and connection. Yet too often obstacles in the form of pressures diminish the meaning and potential. Pressures from demands of family or from the absence of family. Pressures from expectations of the culture, the community and the self about what must be done or felt. Conflicts with work demands. Even more, how does one celebrate amid a world in which there is so much darkness, so many worries, concerns and fears?

It is important that you to reflect not on what is the meaning for others, but for you in your own heart. Let go of your own expectations, the expectations of your culture, and the expectations of those you love. Ask what lies deep in your heart, not on the surface where your heart energies are buffeted by your emotions and your thoughts, but in the quiet and expanded energy of your heart. Your heart holds within it a huge capacity not only to receive and pour forth light and love, but also the capacity to know what is deeply true for you.

When you go to your mind, your mind is crowded with thoughts. Your emotions are noisy. But when you open to the energies of your heart, those energies want to flow. This heart energy wants to communicate to you the truth of who you are. So we would say, if you wish to know the meaning for you, you let go of expectations—those from within and those pressing upon you from the outside. Drop into your own heart with the intention of knowing what is important to you—to the larger expanded you, not the small you.

Your freedom of Being is within you. Always know that. Always know that there is great freedom when you go deeply into your heart. Even if it is just for a few moments, that is where all of you expands and where the fullness of you, the possibility of you, the true you lives and breathes and waits. You are a gift to yourself, waiting to be opened. You are a gift in physical manifestation for the Earth, and you are a gift for your own soul. All that needs to be done is to begin unwrapping this gift.

In this moment, breathe in and allow the love and blessings of those who are around you to protect and assist you, now and always.

Let your heart speak

Anger, frustration, anxiety, fear, disorientation and confusion are being caused by all that is happening in the world—not just the Earth's reactions to all that is damaged and unbalanced but also in the destructive economic, political and military activities. All of that swirls around in the field of the Earth. It swirls around in the larger fields of families, communities, and nations. Where does one go for comfort and understanding in the midst of all the pain and suffering, all the fear and anxiety?

Our counsel is to go into the deepest part of the heart, which is connected to the purest aspect of creation, to the purest aspect of soul. Seek to know the self and the self of the soul. You can reflect from the heart on what you are learning, and what you know that you still want to learn. Lean into the place of inquiry into what you are yearning for, what you are wanting—not in your material life, but what you are wanting for your greater Being.

Let us begin with the assumption that you know, in some way, that you have a soul and you have made a commitment in this life to learn. Because you know you do not begin or end at the boundaries of your skin, learning is about learning your own heart's desire at the deepest level. It is about being willing to be vulnerable to yearning. We do not mean the desire for material things, but that deeper yearning that anchors you to your soul. What is it that you want to experience, to learn from? What is it that opens your heart? What is it that opens your sense of your expanded being?

Let your ego and judgment occupy themselves elsewhere for some moments and allow yourself to be just with yourself, willing to feel the truth of your own being, opening your heart and let what you yearn for speak. Let your deepest heartfelt yearnings come forward. Give voice to that because there is no material requirement for the learning that benefits the soul.

There is no one path. There is no one teacher. There is opening to your heart and letting your heart speak to you and guide you. For within your heart is your deep, deep connection to your soul and your greater being.

It is very scary outside in your world. Take comfort in your ability to take root and nest in the deeper truth of your heart. Your heart is a very safe place and from your heart you can leave the nest and fly with ever greater strength.

Expand your light

This is a time when light needs to expand for everyone who holds a light within—within their being, within their energy field, within their conscious awareness. In the past, there has been fear that to reveal too much, to show too much of the light within would not conform to societal norms and expectations, resulting in punishment rather than reward. There has been fear that there would be conflict rather than peace.

When you present yourself in your truer way, you choose to lead with your light, to let the light guide you, to let the light shine forth, to feel that you are the light. Whatever your job is in the world, your first job is to be the light, wherever you are, with whomever you are with; to hold that light out, not keep it buried inside, though it can feel very good and comforting inside. But now, at this time in your world, the light needs to be held out and up to draw others and let them know that they may also shine their light.

You are not vulnerable because you have so much light to share. Remember the source of that light is the larger you, which is connected directly to your soul. And your soul is connected directly to the Divine, to the source of All. How can there be vulnerability in that? The small self may feel vulnerable. The small self is always plagued by worries about what will be accepted, what will be praised, what will be hurtful to its limited sense of self. It is not that you should abandon the smaller self. Your job is to take care of the body you are in, not with fear, but with light; to be the strength of your own light.

In your world, you turn a switch and the light comes on, and most often that is appreciated. It may seem more complicated to turn on the switch of your own light. But it is not. Trust that if your yearning is to be filled with light, then it will be so. It will be so. Know this. There is much available to you right now to support your stepping out with your light, stepping forward with your light, expanding your light. Ask. Trust. Allow.

Join with the light of others

This is a difficult time in your world and, for most of you, a difficult time in your own personal lives. There are external conditions that create hardships, emotional upheavals, disappointments and many unknowns. We are here to remind you that you are not the small being who experiences these things on your personality level. Yes, your personality is what you put on to go through your life. And yet, if you are reading this, then you know that the personality you are dressed in is not who you are.

It is time to connect to the fullness of your Being, to connect with your Higher Self, the you who remembers connection to the soul's Divine source creation energies, the you who knows unlimited, unconditional love. As this planet and humanity seek to evolve, you are called to expand the light of your Being through direct connection to your higher vibrations of love and to expand the light of your Being by understanding, resolving and integrating the karmic lessons that you've undertaken in this life. This is the way forward for each of you.

As you connect more with your own higher, expanded vibrations of love, compassion and kindness, you grow your ability to reflect on your karmic lessons without the usual emotional patterns or mental thoughts that impede release. When you visit these lessons from your connection to higher vibrations, understanding unfolds more easily, clearing old patterns, energies, thoughts and emotions. This release flows through your entire life journey and forward into your future. This integrated learning and release moves through your entire soul. As you release karmic patterns, you open an ever-clearer pathway to your own highest vibrations.

It truly just takes your focused desire and intention to expand the light of your Being and connect with your own higher vibrations. There are many in spirit who will heed the call of your intention and bring their energies to support your expansion. Your light is needed by humanity and the planet. You are here to allow your light to shine forth so that your light can join with the light of others. You are here to be a blessing to your own self, your own soul, and to others, partly through your actions and words, but also by your Being, your light.

So go forth and be the blessing of light you were made to be.

PART THREE

TEACHINGS FROM THE PEACEKEEPERS

UNDERSTANDING AND ASSISTING THE EVOLUTION OF THE EARTH AND HUMANITY

Resistance to change

We want to provide a message about the urgency of this moment. When we say that there is urgency, it is because we are seeing a pattern of weak energies that need to be strong. We know the strength that will be required in order to manifest the changes that the Earth is moving toward. The more strength there is, the less upheaval there will be. The more awareness there is, the less upheaval there will be. The more acceptance of change, the less upheaval.

We understand that although your entire plane is built upon constant change, there is nevertheless this substantial resistance to the very idea of change. There is the misapprehension that change is destruction. There is the fear that if things are not returned to a previous normal, danger will arise.

Whereas we see that if there is not productive change, if there is not intentional beneficial change, if there is not the acceptance of change for growth and evolution, then there is stagnation, there is decay. Not just physical decay, but moral and energetic decay. A decay in all of the bodies of humanity and all the bodies of the Earth.

So how do we communicate the joy that will arise from embracing an unknown and very changed future? We want to communicate that while you cannot know the future, you can trust that in accepting the changes in your own being, and accepting that the planet must also change, you will come to know a future that will be lighter, better, safer, more fulfilling and easier for all.

Your world is a hard world. Your world is filled with pain and suffering, with acts of violence and betrayals, deceit and injustice. Would you not all want to have a planet where the preponderance of existence for those upon the planet was made up of kindness, love, and generosity, so that when fear arose, love would be there to assist it in calming and relaxing?

When fear arises, it is a trap. It traps the self. It traps other selves. It spreads. But where there is sufficient energy of love, when the frequency of love is strong enough, fear does not grow. It may arise, but it does not expand and grow in the way it does on this plane, your planet now. Wouldn't everyone wish this to be a planet where that was the characteristic of existence?

We understand that we do not speak easy things. We would not have assembled ourselves in this group, which we have created to bring energies of service to the Earth, if this were not a difficult, difficult undertaking; if there was not much to be undone so that the Earth and all its inhabitants can rise to a different plane of existence. There will be those who must leave and there will be those for whom the change will be joyous. But for all those who come forward following the Earth's ascension to its next level, existence will be a very different experience.

Every existence on this planet is beset by the perils of disease, the perils of fear, the perils of anger, the perils of violence. There has been much learning that has come because of the nature of this planet, but it is time for those lessons to end. It is time for new lessons and a new classroom—one that is filled with light. We are here in the service of this great change.

The Earth needs to evolve

We are watching what is happening in the Earth energies. What we are seeing is an increasing amount of fear, anxiety, violence, desperation. There is much desperation. This is a very distorting energy when it is put forward into the energetic field. It is a disrupter. It is a disrupter for individuals and a disrupter for communities.

Whenever an individual is putting forth the energy of desperation, there has been a degrading of the spirit; a weakening of their connection to others and to their own higher self. There is no desperation when there is connection to the higher energies or the actual Earth energies.

So yes, we are seeing this energy of desperation permeating many places. The Earth has come to a point where it cannot sustain the initiating vibrations that it was intended to create within. The Earth evolves. You think of the evolution of species and the diversity of biological forms. But this is not, of course, the whole of the Earth's evolution. Just as your physical form grows, matures, ages and then begins to degrade, so in cosmic time will the young Earth's physical form. But the physical form is only one aspect. The soul of the Earth is evolving just as your own souls are evolving. The energy that the soul of the Earth is seeking to bring forward now as part of the evolution of the Earth is of higher vibrations. These vibrations will enable those who embody on this new Earth to understand, to see and to live where there is vibrational energetic support, both in how they are embodied and in the Earth itself, for the states of peace, love, kindness, compassion, gentleness.

It is not that there will be no conflict, differences. There are always those things. But what is the energy that conflicts call forth? Differences and conflicts now call forth anger, shunning, dismissal, rage, confusion. The Earth's evolved vibrations will evoke more tolerance, curiosity, and exploration of how to move forward with differences. The Earth will continue to be a planet with its emphasis on individuality, but individuality with awareness of connection, and greater ease of connection.

The 'new' Earth will create greater peaceful prospects for all, not only for those embodying on the Earth, but also for the many beings whose existences and homes are far from the Earth and yet part of the whole. With the Earth on a different vibrational plane, there will be greater safety and greater protection for the Earth and its inhabitants. When the vibrations of the Earth are less volatile, less dense, Earth will not attract the denser entities that are present in the universes of beings.

We want people on the Earth to rise up and claim peace. Claim the desire for peace. It is in everyone. Somewhere in everyone is the desire for a peaceful life, a kind life; the desire for more gentleness and connection to others. Those desires, when allowed expression with hope, assist the Earth in raising its vibration. And those who cannot find any of that inside them will be called home, but not necessarily in a way that they would choose.

So this is a time when there cannot be delay. When we say that this is the time we do not mean this hour or this day or even this year. But to amass the energies that are needed to birth the ascension of the Earth and individuals takes great persistence and fortitude over an extended period. And in your terms of time there cannot now be delay, or the consequences for everyone will become increasingly painful in terms of their experience on the Earth. Life on Earth will become increasingly difficult for everyone, no matter what vibration they are able to manifest.

We are the voice of urgency here. It is urgent. Individuals must step forward now.

Assist the Earth in its healing

We want to make a distinction between what one does as an individual on the planet to raise their vibration in the ways that are personally beneficial and what one can do to feed the energies that will assist the planet Earth in its healing and in the raising of the vibration of the planet overall. As you already know, when the vibration of the planet is raised, this has a direct effect on those who are on the planet. As the raising of the vibration of the planet occurs, those who are not comfortable and able to be at peace with the higher vibration will move on, reconnecting with their essence. Their experience of the change in vibration will be a learning that they take back with them to their essence, helping them to prepare for the next time that the essence is put forward into embodiment.

What we want you to note is that there are layers to this. And even as you work on your own vibrational changes, the work to assist the planet must be ongoing. An occasional thought will not make the difference. An article will not make the difference, although an article that was read by millions, who then embraced an ongoing practice of working to raise the vibration of the planet, would be valuable. We are saying that while it is not a full-time job for the hands and feet, a full-time conscious awareness is needed to imbue the whole being with the purpose of planetary ascension. Your purpose could be to serve as a person who puts out fires and yet, at the same time, you can also be a person who does everything with an awareness of assisting the planet in its healing and transition to a higher vibration.

We understand that this may be confusing for you. Yet it is not confusing for you when you are working with people, living your life with others. Have you not had separate jobs and tasks, but still held an awareness of others even when it was not required to complete the work? You are at work or doing your errands and yet you are holding an awareness of others who are not present: their feelings, their heart, their potential, their needs. Sometimes it may be forward and sometimes it may have been lurking, but it was always there. It is the same with this idea of planetary healing. It is another focus for your multi-tasking.

While we are talking about planetary ascension, we use the term planetary healing because this is more accessible. Everyone understands, or thinks they understand, healing. Everyone thinks they understand the things that are making the planet sick. And so 'planetary healing' is a set of words that are approachable. Planetary ascension is a more cumbersome, difficult concept. The planet's ascension to a higher vibrational state is what the ultimate healing will be.

If something is wrong with the physical body, you work to cure that. But because of what was wrong in one part, other parts of the body become distressed. And because of that, the emotional state of the being is distressed. And because of that, the mind becomes fuzzy. And so you may cure the first thing, but you have not healed the body. You have not healed the person. You have only dealt with the visible injury or disease.

Just so with the planet. Even if you could cure all the visible injuries, which we think you cannot, it would not heal the planet because the planet is mired in so many layers of lower vibrations that are not beneficial. So there is a need for healing that changes the vibrations surrounding the planet. When there is clearing, when there is a change to a higher vibration, then the planet will indeed be healed from the deepest core outward and up through the etheric levels.

From those who have conscious awareness, much is needed and much is required. Being of service to the planet in this responsible way, there is much growth in the essence of the being. To be in the body, living in a body on the planet and taking on the responsibility of heightened awareness and commitment to change, to healing for the planet, that type of service is very beneficial for the expansion of the essence, what you call the soul of the being.

The Earth is your home

We think it is very important that people on Earth begin to think of the planet as their home. This may seem like an obvious concept, but it is not obvious. While some people are slovenly in their upkeep of their home, many, many people care about their home. They care about it, no matter how meager their resources, how limited their ability to care for themselves or the surrounding environment of their home. Even those you call homeless, they have a home: their home is Earth. And on this Earth, perhaps only they have a box and some plastic and whatever they have acquired. But even among those who you call homeless, there are those who are careful about how they maintain their box.

Yes, so even those who have very little can take great care because it is what they call home. It is where they live. And these same people who can take care of their home, keeping it clean and neat with everything in what they consider to be the right place, they do not understand that Earth is their home. It is their Earth. They are those who live in this home. If that knowing were part of the consciousness of each one when they were born and as they grew up and became independent adults, much could change. Much can change. We offer that as one of the first steps.

As we understand it, there is currently a notion of disruption as beneficial and we would agree, because change is part of growth. For example, a change in understanding disrupts what has been accepted, it disrupts how one has thought. And that is very important. Changing the understanding of the Earth as your home disrupts the current distance between the individual and the Earth, allowing the meaning to penetrate. Take all your common phrases about home and think of the Earth.

Lift your vibration

We want to address the subject of how people view their environment. Because how one views the world, the environment in which one is planted and in which one moves, affects many, many things. Often you have the feeling that you are in your environment, wherever you happen to be, and you are just in your skin, in your individual being, and that is all that matters—that is where you are focused and moving through your activities. But without awareness of the environment outside your skin, you are making yourself vulnerable.

You are now very aware that when people cough, they send into the environment things that were within them that could be harmful to you if you were to breathe it in. But what you are not understanding is that when you are withdrawn into your skin and not aware of your environment—and we are not talking now about the viruses or germs in the environment, but about the energies in the environment—then you are walking around completely unaware of what you are sending out into the environment for others to absorb, or what your energy field is having to absorb from others.

If you had a sickness on your skin, you would notice, would you not? Yes, you would notice. But when you have not a sickness, but energies that are not beneficial in your energy field, you are not aware until they become so dense that they begin to affect your physical body. These may be energies that you are putting forth, which are not only going out into the world, but also into your own energy field, or they may be energies of others that you have been absorbing without attention.

We know that not everyone realizes their ability to be aware of the environment in which they are moving and the environment to which they are adding energies. But this is a very important skill. This is why there are now many, many groups that are trying to help people learn to pay attention to what you could call the psychic environment, the etheric environment, the energetic environment; to pay attention to their intuition, which says there are energies here that I do not want. Well, that is one side, but before you even get to that, you have the ability to be aware of your own energies, of how you are feeling and what you are putting into the energetic atmosphere.

When you are going through your activities in a state of aggravation, do you think that that aggravation is only yours? No, you are putting it out, you are sharing it. Even if you are silent, you are sharing it. And when you are not silent about it, then you are just emphasizing that energy and giving it more strength, sending it out more forcefully. But even when you are not speaking, you are sending it out, you are radiating it, because that is how emotions work. When you send out love, you send out a vibration, a frequency. When you feel joy, you are sending out that vibration. When you feel anger, you are sending out a vibration, a frequency of anger that goes into the environment. So, yes, you are walking through a soup of energies. Just as you would care what kind of soup you ate, so you should care about what kind of soup you are walking through and what you are contributing to the soup.

When you are walking around and you are feeling gratitude, kindness, generosity, love, those vibrations move out and have a beneficial effect. Think of them as an antibiotic. Yes, those vibrations are the antibiotic that works to heal the infections created by the energies of anger and despair and sadness and depression. Because in the end, it is not that those feelings and states are bad in themselves. This is not about good and bad. It is about frequency and vibration and the vibrations that benefit physical health, that benefit planetary health, that benefit communal health. You would not see a seriously depressed person and think, oh, what a picture of health. They may indeed need, for their own soul purposes, to work through their depression, their sadness, their unexpressed anger because there are learnings there for them. But a depressed planet would not be a healthy place to live. An angry planet where that is the primary vibration would not be a healthy place for living things, certainly not healthy for the planet itself.

You care about being healthy on some level. And you care about living in a place that is healthy for you. So one small thing you can do is to be aware first of how you are feeling. When you are aware, you can choose what you are sending out into the atmosphere and that others will be affected by it.

We do not mean that you should not be sad. No, because sadness is rich in learning opportunities. But what we are suggesting is to find the place in you that wants to see beauty. Find the place in you that is grateful. Grateful for the sky, grateful for the tree, grateful for the color that you see, grateful for the what the senses are giving you.

Particularly when you are out in the presence of others, find in yourself a true place, yes, what you call an authentic place, but one where you are not sending out your sadness. You have changed the lens. You will come back to the lens of sadness because it is important for you perhaps. Or the lens of anger or the part of you that is depressed and is trying to understand what is giving rise to that. But find the place in you that can focus on the small thing that lifts the vibration that you are sending out. That is beneficial for you, beneficial for others and beneficial for the planet, because each time a higher vibration is put out into the environment, it accumulates. It is very beneficial for everyone to try, as much as possible, to allow higher vibrations, healthier vibrations to rise.

You carry the seeds of the future

We want to provide additional information about what evolution means for a species. When you think of evolution in your terms, you see small changes that are adaptations to an environment. Sometimes a mutation happens, and that mutation is successful and then through procreation there are more with the mutation until that difference, that mutation, begins to take over and become the template for the species going forward until the next mutation occurs that is beneficial and that then predominates. That is the general sense of what is meant by evolution for your planet and for the life forms on your planet.

There are ways in which what is possible for humankind is, in a sense, that type of evolution. You have many, many more on your planet who are coming forward with a recognition of the unseen energies that move across your planet and the unseen energies that move out from themselves, which they can access and from which they can access information. As the number of humans capable of achieving this level of awareness increases, that changes the environment of the Earth's energies, the larger energy surrounding the human species. In your third-dimension terms, it becomes an environmental shift. And that environmental shift then allows even more humans to come forward with more awareness of the unseen energies. So that is one way of seeing what we are talking about in terms of the evolution of the human species.

What is complicated to explain is that you are one species on one planet in an ever larger and larger container; an ever larger and larger cycle of evolution, change, creation. So just as you are evolving, the Earth's energies are also evolving, because the humans who are coming in are aided by more energy of awareness. In this way that energy of awareness becomes part of the Earth's environment, not just for the human species, but for the Earth itself.

Just as humans evolve, planets evolve in their essence, in the essence of the energies that surround them. When the planet evolves it also evolves to another dimension. That means that how one interacts with the Earth, what the Earth affords, how all the things on the Earth are formed and change, that also is part of evolution. So when the planet is able to make the transition to the next dimension for its path, how it expresses in that dimension will be different. And because how it expresses is different, because the energies that are a part of it are now changed, when souls incarnate as human and become embodied with their purposes, the energies around which and through which those purposes will be pursued will be very different.

Here on this planet, this plane, this dimension, you must pursue your purposes with limited sight. There is a certain inability to see because so much of seeing is on the fixed forms, the dense forms. So much of what is experienced is in a dense form: dense emotions, dense thoughts. On the next plane that is the potential for the human species, how one perceives will be very different. What one perceives will not be that things are separate, divided. Perception will be supported by abundant resources for understanding and knowing connection. There will be embodiments where there are difficulties around accepting connection. But that is very different than being on a plane where *all* is disconnection and where the struggle to find a connection, to find meaningful connection on every level is a considerable test.

It will remain a test on the next plane, but with many more resources, different resources; not the resources of opposition, but the resources of support and understanding and being able to see and know much more that reinforces the knowing of connection, the knowing of love, the knowing of wholeness. This next step is far from the place where there is union and where there is openness and fullness in the knowing of oneness. But it is a great step forward for the human species.

In your terms, you are now on the third dimensional plane and the possibility for the human species on the planet is to evolve to the fifth dimensional plane. It is important to remember that all these terms are just words that are put to these other experiences of existing. We do not communicate with words, though that is happening now. Our communication happens through energies.

What is communicating in this way like? We can give you an image. When you want comfort from someone you trust and love, and they open their arms and embrace you fully, and as they embrace you, you feel their love, you feel their caring and it warms you, releasing some level of sadness or fear or worry that you were holding. Instead, in those moments, you feel held, supported, loved, understood, cared for. That fullness, because you are being embraced, it is all of you, yes? All of you takes in that love: your skin takes it in, your mind takes it in, your eyes take it in, your ears take it in, your whole body takes it in. Mind, emotion, body and even your spirit takes in that love.

When we are communicating, it is not that those emotions predominate, but there is that sense of fullness of accepting; that opening to accepting and then the feeling of the fullness. That type of energetic fullness and connection in communication holds the essence of what existing within a higher dimensional plane affords.

This is something to look forward to, although we understand that many of you reading this will not be present in your current form when this possibility arises. But those of you who are aware and who have many years before you will be present for the birthing of this evolution. In a sense, those of you who have already mutated and begun to open those channels, those receptors for receiving energetic communication and knowing and integrating, you will see that you are becoming the majority. And you will see how the Earth changes in response to your energies and the accumulation of all of you with this new form of awareness and communication. Because as that new vibration moves into the Earth's atmosphere, into your field and out into the larger field of the human species, it will even affect all the other living things.

Those who have not yet opened to this evolutionary process will be less successful. There will be—to call them battles is not correct. There will be fear, because when things change and one person or one part of the species is able to do something that the others cannot do, there can be conflict. But in the end, it is about not just who is successful in the environment. It is about the nature of creation and the larger cycles. Evolution, change, growth, these are the cycles of creation energy and they move to ever higher levels of energetic expression that become closer and closer to the pure Source energy of creation.

All of us have within us this incredible creation energy. You carry yours, but it is as if you do not know it is there. Or you begin to use it, but you do not know what you are using. You have this amazing tool, but you are not using it for its true purpose or to its fullest extent, or to even a tiny amount of its potential.

Think of all the precious metals, stones that your planet creates naturally. For eons no use was made of those materials. It took knowing that the materials were there to begin to uncover how they might assist in living. Just so, you have this creation energy. You have it, but because you are in a dense form, many are not aware of it and it is of no use to your consciousness.

But as you evolve, as your consciousness opens up, as your awareness and receptors to receiving energies increase, then your knowing of the creation energy becomes greater, and its expression in you and in the environment grows. With each movement in the cycle of growth to the next plane, the next dimension, the creation energy becomes even greater, even stronger, even, we could say, more pure—by which we mean it is less and less dense, less and less fixed, more and more fluid.

And so here you are at this very important moment in a cycle of growth; in a cycle of evolution; in a cycle of opening to ever more. It is a very important time. You all carry the gene of the future of the human species in you. You are part of the change that is happening. You are part of enabling it to happen. The future of your species depends on you. And all you have to do is continue to open to your own ability to be aware and to know. You are creating the future by how you think and what you offer through your energies.

Fear is strong, love is stronger

Our messages carry urgency because the lower density energies that are moving across the Earth are increasing. This increase in the denser energies can be understood as an aspect of change. One thing begins to grow and another thing begins to grow in reaction. But one is growing through hope and love. The other is growing through fear.

On your planet fear is incredibly powerful. It has power everywhere, but on your planet fears are actively perpetuated, evoked, and nurtured into becoming ever greater fears; whereas though love is much spoken of on your planet it is not nourished in the same way. It is, on your plane, viewed as more fragile. There are many ideas about the fragility of love and these thoughts and ideas carry weight, ignoring the vibration of higher love. The vibration that is named love, for our purposes of communication, that vibration is the strongest that is available, not just on your planet, but everywhere. It is the primary platform of life.

At this moment, it is important that all who are capable of expanding their heart, expanding and touching love's strength, the powerful vibration that is love—all those who can do this, approach, intend, and desire this—need to join with others who are like-hearted and light-hearted. Be present to those times when there is the intention to send out love, to send out love to all living things, to expand the heart to be stronger, so much stronger than the waves of fear and sadness and grief that arise.

Love must rise. That vibration must be nourished. We are here trying to do our part in nourishing that vibration for your planet. But when you who have bodies, who are connected and anchored to this planet, when you send this higher energy—when you open to this higher energy, when you release this energy, letting it flow through you and out through you to all—when you do that, the impact is substantial. Do not doubt this. Find others. Join together, whether it is in person or on your screens, whether it is in the moment or you are participating in a recording with others, know that the energy is there.

When there is the intention, that intention stays activated, particularly when a new intention participates with the gathered intention. Is that understood? You have meditation books and videos, and tapes. When you are reading or watching or listening, you are alone. But if the meditation, if the guided journey, if the words—the channeled words or the words of the human being—are put forward with the intention of sending forth a higher vibration of love and healing, of generating and evoking those energies and sending those vibrations out into the world, then you add to that intention and those energies. Your participation further activates the intentions and the energies of all who read, listened or watched previously. These collective intentions go into a resource, a pool. Each time more join, the pool grows. But also it is like a pebble dropping in water and the wave of that energy moving out again, but now with additional energy. So however you can join with others, it is beneficial to do so.

And do not delay, because it will only extend the pain and the suffering.

We who watch your planet do so with great love and great understanding of all that is before you that is so light, so free. And yet we are also understanding all the darkness that currently seems to be in the way. But you must trust. Trust in the power of the higher vibrations of love. Trust in the power of healing. Trust in the power of your own intention to be part of the evolution of the human and the Earth to a new platform of being.

We will be here with you. Many, many of us will be with you through this entire transition, calling to all who are awake or who may be awakened to this momentous time in the journey of the human and the Earth.

A difficult transformation

Your entire planet is in the midst of a difficult transformation. Even as the higher vibrations increase on and around the Earth, the denser, darker, heavier vibrations and energies grow fear, anger, hate. It may seem as if your planet is at the point of being overrun with darkness. There have always been denser, heavier vibrations in this dimension. It is part of the expression of the planet's dimensional existence and the conditions that exist in a third-dimensional reality. But just as there is darkness, there has always been light. It is the light that drives the Earth's and humanity's larger purposes and their evolution; the belief in love, kindness, generosity and oneness that lights the way forward.

You are part of an evolution to lighter densities and higher vibrations. And so we are asking that you hold within you the desire to evolve. We ask that you hold within your being a passion for humanity's evolution to a higher dimension of being. We ask that you hold the belief that the planet Earth can also evolve to its next dimension, supporting higher vibrations and nourishing embodied beings.

We speak of the higher vibrations of the heart, the higher vibrations of knowing, the expansion of mind, the experience of connection, of being in the embrace of the whole, of knowing your being within that whole. This is a different way of being, and it is what lies before you. But you must choose to go through this time not with hate, not with anger, not with weapons, not with aggression but with love and kindness, with your own higher vibrations.

The more you nurture your own higher vibrations, your own kindness, your own generosity, your own expansion into those experiences of love, kindness, generosity, opening to others, that is what will bring forward the light and vanquish that which seeks to prevent the evolution of you, of humanity, of the Earth. It is time for you to believe in the power of your own ability to be greater than you think you are.

Open pathways to higher vibrations

When there is news in your media about galaxies and universes, these are moments when minds open to different ideas and energies. When there is a closed mind, there is no opportunity to raise the vibration and as we have said, this is a time when what is needed is for the vibrations surrounding the Earth to be raised to a higher level and frequency.

When there is opening to ideas, to thoughts and to feelings that are larger than just the single individual on their narrow path, those are moments when the frequency for the individual may expand. And so when there is news that speaks to the stars, then that is a moment when those who are already attuned to opening to higher frequencies, to the need for the Earth's frequencies to be raised, to redouble their efforts.

Even if those who are reading the news are not consciously thinking, 'Oh, my mind is opening,' nevertheless it is happening and that opening can be used. The field of energy in those moments is available to be coalesced into joy. When thinking about life and the possibilities of the universe, there is an energy of anticipation, curiosity, we might even call it love. Those are words that take you to a higher vibration.

Even an idea has a frequency, and ideas that open up the mind have a higher frequency, so they are like a springboard. It is as if you have a net and you are capturing all these energies that are springing up, pushing them up into the field and expanding them. In this way you are leveraging the news and its effect upon people, not to the people who have fear, but to the people who have interest. And you push that up into the Earth's field, into the larger energetic field, because you want to open the doorway, to open the pathways for higher frequencies and higher vibrations.

It is about intention. There are many energies pressing down on the Earth. Your intention is to capture a moment and use it to increase the open space around the planet so that the Earth can breathe. That higher frequency is the Earth's right, needed not just by the Earth, but by the universe within which the Earth exists.

We want those of you who are interested in supporting the Earth in its ascension to be on the watch for those moments when you can choose to use positive momentum. Yes, it's true that right now there is much conflict, but one can focus not on the conflict and the tensions, but on the openings for peace, the opening of minds, the opening of hearts, the opening of ideas and expressions. Every person contributes, every being and their energies contribute to the state of the Earth. So, yes, you start with your own being, but then you look for how you can expand beyond your own being in helping to raise the vibrations for the Earth and humanity.

In our group, we have all come from existences where the evolution of consciousness depended on vibrational states and awareness. While it may be far in the past for us, still that learning and those processes are present as if they were taking place now. We appreciate the difficulty, we understand the pain, we know the rewards, and we feel the urgency.

Open hearts guide the way

We come today to speak more about the energies of movement from one plane or dimension of being to another. It is not like your elevators, though we know you use this metaphor. That would be a smooth and easy transition from level one to level two, but that is not the best metaphor for the transition from one plane to the next. We think perhaps the image of climbing a mountain might be more appropriate.

When a mountain is being climbed, there is much effort. There is the need for focus. There is the need for clarity of purpose. There are risks that arise from inattention and there are risks even when the attention and focus are strong. One is not in isolation. One climbs with others and one climbs upon something that has its own component parts. There are stronger and weaker elements. If you put your trust on a weaker element, the risk of falling, of injury is increased.

The process of ascension is one that takes a multitude climbing the mountain at the same time. While everyone is not following the same path, all are focused on moving in the same direction. They share the same goal. Some will tire and give up, but as more and more achieve higher levels toward the summit, there is more hope and inspiration for those who are still further below. But all are joined in the process, as if there were a rope that each climber holds so that the movement and the slackening can be felt by all.

There are limits to the metaphor of course, but you see that this is a process like mountain climbing, which requires great effort. Only when the majority reach the top can the summit become the new home. Of course, in time, one discovers the next mountain with an even higher summit and the energy for a new climb begins to gather.

As beings who have in our own histories experienced the ascension of our homes and of our species, we are here to assist your planet and humanity in this arduous and wondrous task of ascending to new vibrational capacities. We want to share what we know from our own histories and from what we can see in the current energies surrounding the Earth and the human fields.

There is always resistance to change, because those vested in the structures and morals and principles that have been in place and in power are loathe to give up their standing. Our civilization was not one of warring across territories but there were certainly tensions and conflicts between new ideas and old ones, new principles for approaching problems and older ones. There has always been, across all ways of being, the possibility of power and authority becoming stratified and rigidified. But in our experiences, which were not as concretely physicalized as humanity's, there were energy shifts that were openly in play. We do not have access to words from your concepts to explain the experience of those with less density of form. Our beings have always had less density of form than the human template because of the nature of the creation impulse originating our home stars and planets.

We know from our histories that the important tools you bring to climbing the ascension mountain lie within your hearts and in your ability to hope and expand your heart energies. As you open your heart energies as a main focus, no matter what you are doing, you send forth a vibration into your field. When you do this, you connect with the resonance of your own higher heart. When you activate this element of your own field of energies it is a welcome sign. When you do this, a higher and less dense energy is emitted from your field out into the larger field of human communication. This energy has the ability to penetrate the fields of others. Think of it as a whisper, a light touch of the higher energies of others, which then flows back toward the denser elements of the human and perhaps touches the consciousness, even if not recognized.

This is the slow process of eliciting ever more participation in the movement toward the summit. It takes nothing more than holding love forward, which is in truth a big undertaking.

In your world there are times and places where love is acceptable in expression. There are other times, places and circumstances where it is not allowed or is devalued. For some there is risk in expressing love because it is viewed as a weakness. For some the fear of being hurt cancels out their ability to express love.

Fear is the greatest enemy of love. So to be a good ascension climber you must meet and reconcile all that you fear. We can tell you that love is the strongest vibration there is, because it has the power of creation energies as its source and ongoing fuel. We can tell you that you have an incredible reservoir of love available to you and that each time you tap that reservoir it is not lessened but expands.

The Earth is powerful and has a path toward higher planes. But the Earth came into being to be a place for souls to incarnate and human beings became the path. Thus, the Earth depends on you even as you have always depended on it. Do you see that the planet is an embodiment, an expression of a huge amount of creation energy with a drive to continue to evolve and develop? The Earth developed first in its physical manifestation and in its changing, evolving physical expressions. Then it was joined by humans and together—in harmony and not—they have each continued to evolve.

The Earth has been ready for some time to make further steps toward ascension but has been held back by humanity's attachment to the denser energies. However, that has now begun to shift. That is why the Earth's expressions of healing, throwing off aspects in order to lighten the load, you would say, is in process. The Earth's energies move from the core outward, as do your own. They also move from the energetic field and the physical field around and inward and the two either resonate and reinforce or come into temporary stasis.

It is time now for humans to understand their joint journey with the Earth in much larger terms. We will offer ways to approach understanding and sensing this essential relationship, which serves the mutual benefit of the planet and all of humanity. We will offer suggestions on how to equip yourself for the climb ahead.

But first we want to talk about the Earth's energies during the ascension transition. Think of it this way. The Earth is climbing its own mountain to reach a new higher dimension. Earth must not only adjust all her previous creations to reach the new dimension and to be in alignment with it, but it must carry the whole of humanity with her. This is why you have been told it is a partnership. If humans do not participate, the weight of their denser energies will suppress the Earth's evolution.

Your thoughts have power

Our message about the planet is that difficulties are being caused by human responses to the Earth's attempts to find balance in energies that are being depleted. Think of reservoirs of water, or forests as reservoirs of nourishment. These physical reservoirs are being removed and depleted by human activity. Like the depletion of its physical resources, the Earth's energy is being depleted.

Just like you, the Earth's life force energies need to be nourished. What balances your energy when you are feeling depleted? If you are feeling sad or depressed, what can lift you out of that? Well, positive thoughts, joy. That which makes you laugh, that which makes you feel loved, that which makes you feel cared about. That which is gentle, that which is soft—all your terms for ways of giving and receiving different nourishing energies. So when what is triggered in humanity is anger and sadness and fear, then those energies join with the physical manifestations of drought, of storm, of earthquake, of eruptions. And then Earth has even more to cope with and no one to help.

We understand that it may seem simplistic to think about your thoughts having power. Certainly your actions have had a great deal of power in depleting the Earth. And your actions now to try to assist the Earth are very meager, despite many of you wanting to do better. But what everyone can do is to stop the fear. Stop the anger, stop the sadness, and instead send the Earth love, send the Earth compassion, send the Earth your joy in what you still see around you that raises your spirit. Look for those things of the Earth that raise your spirit and send that uplift back to the Earth.

You cannot replant all the forests. You cannot bring back all the rainforests. You cannot bring back all the water that once was clean and now is polluted. However, you can contribute to the energies surrounding the Earth, those that flow both down into the Earth and those that flow up into the Earth's field. We know it is difficult for many of you to accept that each of your thoughts goes out into the atmosphere. Are your thoughts polluting your own field? Are they polluting the Earth's field?

Maybe you are one who takes care of how you dress because you want to be seen as someone who is thoughtful or careful or organized or clean. Pay as much attention to what you think, what you feel, what you put out into your field and what you send out into the Earth's field. That is what you can do.

We watch those who understand the power of intention. Intention matters. Align your thoughts with your intention and align whatever acts you can with that intention. Keep reinforcing the idea, the thought. There is reason to continue to be hopeful but only if those of you who are sufficiently aware can manage to integrate into your being the importance of regulating what you are sending out from your being into the atmosphere, into the field of the Earth and indeed into your own field, into the energy of your home, into the energetic field wherever you are.

Let it be simple. Find your way. Find your way because the Earth depends on you. We who are not on the Earth plane can send guidance, can send our own energies, but the power of all the embodied beings on the surface of the planet carries so much weight. It is for your own good, not just the good of the Earth. There is so much beauty in what may be. Believe in that.

Attend to what needs clearing

The changes in the human energy field are a vital component of the ascension process. The field for most humans even now is very dense and mostly activated in those layers or bands that move closest to the physical body. In these components there reside the most accumulation of denser, older, less welcomed thoughts, emotions and physical memories. These are all residues and they are sticky and not always easy to clean away.

They do serve a purpose in foregrounding what remains to be learned. So while it is beneficial to sweep these layers free of clutter, what doesn't get swept away needs to be examined, understood, reconciled and then dissolved into an integrated learning or set of learnings. If these layers remain dense and weighted, it makes it difficult for the individual to reach their own higher vibrations. Since the ultimate attainment of a new level or plane of existence is dependent on connection with the higher vibrations within the individual's field, as well as connection with the larger human field of vibrations, the clearing of these residues is an essential step for each person.

The soul, in creating the template for the embodiment, knows the residues that will arise or be embedded so that the most important learning can be achieved. There are many layers to the soul's purposes in any one embodiment; one layer is the clearing up of what remains to be learned and integrated based on the soul's progress and intentions. Participation in larger purposes such as ascension is another layer of purpose. And there are always soul-to-soul agreements related to connections with others—with helpers, guides and teachers, both physically embodied and in spirit.

When the innermost and denser layers of the human etheric field are cleared and lightened, then the connection to the higher energies and vibrations can be developed. We speak here of the individual's intentional connection to their greater heart, their expanded consciousness and their connection to the higher spiritual energies. You can think of this as beginning to tune to different frequency bands. You have experience with your radio waves, where you search for the stations that you can reach and you seek to have a clear connection, not a fuzzy one. There are narrower bands and wider ones. There are higher frequencies and lower ones, stronger and weaker radio waves, and adjacencies that affect the strength of your reception.

Once the lower energies are cleared, the ability to move out and connect to higher vibrations opens. With greater intention and focus, the strength of the 'signal' increases. Based on previous experiences in connecting with these energies in past embodiments, and the attunements that the soul has embedded into the template for this lifetime, the strength and ease of connecting are shaped.

If you are reading these words, then your soul has already preset the possibility for a strong connection with your own higher vibrations. You carry in your field the template for these vibrations. Activation is one of the tasks you have been in the process of undertaking.

What the ascension requires is even more activation of your own higher vibrations. Once your higher energies are open and activated and you are able to connect with your higher heart energies, your higher consciousness vibrations and your higher spiritual energies, then you can both receive and send those energies out to the greater field that surrounds humanity.

Remember that all is connected. What you send out, unintentionally and intentionally, flows into the energetic field encompassing all of humanity. It is one field. Though composed of many elements, yet all is connected. This is where an energetic experience of higher heart, mind and soul energies becomes difficult to put into words.

Becoming aware of what you are putting into the larger field is an important next step. What do you want to breathe in? What do you want to move into your field, into your skin, to allow into your being? You may set up protections to guard against those vibrations and energies that you do not want to pollute your field. You also do not want to add pollutants to the fields of others.

When you have opened your own higher vibrations to any extent, you then have created a channel for receiving more of those energies, more support for the expansion of your field as those vibrations move into all of you. You are a seemingly solid body or core surrounded by many layers of an energy atmosphere. Energies flow from the body out through the field and beyond, even as energies from the outside move into the layers of the field and into the heart of the embodied being.

Can you imagine or sense this process of clearing, opening, flowing and fine tuning, with you becoming an ever more expanded receiver and transmitter? Do you see that you are a sphere of energy?

Connecting to the greater whole

We will focus on providing more information on the meaning of that term ascension. You are familiar with it, and many who are already engaged in spiritual connection are familiar with it, because of the connection to the term 'Ascended Masters,' meaning those who have gone beyond a limited sense of self or being and have the capacity to connect with the greater All. They have shed, you could say, many of the barriers to being more completely whole and more consciously connected to being a part of the greater whole. The Ascended Masters are beings who operate energetically, not within physical form. Their souls are on an evolutionary path as beings having infinite possibility for connection because they have the capacity to connect to the greatest of energies. This is not easy to put into your words because it is an experience of being, not an experience of thinking.

When you think of Ascended Masters you are still linking them with a human identification, like Kuan Yin and Master Buddha and Jesus. You have these beings who at one point were connected to the Earth and for whom the Earth is still a focus of their purpose. That is, they have purposes related to teaching. These are master teachers, you could say. They themselves could simply merge into the light of creation, but they have chosen instead to use that capacity for merging, their knowing of the All, as the foundational energy for their teaching on the Earth.

We are not focused on the Earth. All the beings present in The Peacekeeper group have been part of an evolutionary process that has moved to less and less density, more and more fluidity. We have evolved more capacity for connection and energetic linking; and an expansion of knowing, which we think of as sharing, that allows us to operate in this realm of communicating with beings in different locations, as you think of it.

We understand ascending as becoming less and less dense, less and less constricted and contained. That is, the frequencies and pathways for communication and connection open and expand with fewer boundaries and greater capacity across time and distance. It is not that we are one with all of those in our evolutionary heritage and group. But we have an ability to share and connect across all of those that we are a part of, as well as with others who come from other evolutionary processes that started in different places, with their own course of development.

You can think of our process of as becoming lighter and more fluid. This means that when we are connecting with energies across planetary groups who have a similar evolutionary process of ascending into higher vibrational connections, we can communicate because there is an openness to sharing through the resonances of experiences and learning and connections to the greater All.

Perhaps this is not so helpful for those of you on Earth who are trying to understand why ascension matters. But that is the process. Most of those on Earth now are still operating from that place of density of form. But others of you have opened to what you call the light, to that sense of connection to something greater, whether it is only to the sense of connecting to your own soul, your home energy, or whether you are opening to other vibrations that connect to what you think of as healing energies. When you have that opening in you, then indeed you have the capacity to share at higher vibrational levels such as the channel is doing now.

When this channel is in her daily routine there might be an energetic knock on the door, so to speak, and she might attend to it or not, but in those moments she is opening even briefly to different vibrational levels in her own capacity. And that is a way of lessening the density and increasing the vibrational frequency to be at a higher level.

When you have even the tiniest spark of connection to energies that are larger and outside of the skin, then there is a release of a certain level of density, holding in, constraining. When that lightening occurs, it allows energy that is less dense, lighter, somewhat higher in frequency to go out into your atmosphere, and be beneficial for the whole. It is beneficial for the being because now there is an opening; and for the soul energies, this is a release into more expansion and more connection. Once it is begun, there is greater ease in opening further, expanding further. This benefits the self in the body, it benefits the soul, it benefits the whole of the species.

This is the evolutionary process, and as more of you open to it, you become the template for the species. And that is really what ascension means at this point in the evolutionary pattern for Earth and humanity.

See yourself as the carrier of the vibration, the energy, we could call it the gene, that will then be perpetuated. More and more humans need to open to higher vibrations so that the dominant template can become one of less density, higher vibration, higher frequency.

You are a part of the multiverse

We want to put the meaning of ascension in the context of the greater whole, that is, all that exists outside of your planet and species because, indeed, we are representatives of those other forms and places of being. We have all, in different processes and different phases of change, evolved from an originating energy and form and manner of acting, communicating, changing. We have all, through eons and eons of time in your counting, reached these levels of vibration where we can travel distances in our thoughts and purposes and we can commingle at an energetic level for purposes of communication and joint projects. Our interests are not our own planets or systems or species, but the whole, because we are all benefited when every part of the whole is in alignment with, we could say, higher purposes, meaning that which recognizes an energy of wholeness.

All of us in this group have gone through our own versions of what the Earth is going through. Our species moved through different phases of development in ascending to our current expressions of being that allow us to serve the greater whole. When the Earth is gripped in darkness, that darkness is part of the whole. And as your technologies advance, your moral sense does not; your fears and the actions they trigger become ever more dangerous. Our concern for the well-being of the whole is increasing, not just for your planet and people but for the whole.

These are difficult times, but there has already begun a movement within humanity toward a lighter, less dense energy. You see the reactions to change. For decades you have watched changes occurring and the fight against those changes that are about including, not dividing; connecting, not separating; about accepting all humans with love not just tolerating them with disdain. From our perspective, these changes and the energies they carry represent what is more beneficial and safer for all. Because these energies have been coming in and are growing, we are present to add our counsel and our energies.

As you already know, when our energies come forward through a human, the energy that we are sending moves out into the Earth and through to other humans. The connection with a human vibration carrying our energies is very helpful. When we are just sending our energies into your atmosphere for the purposes of providing more support for the lighter, higher vibrations, those who are already attuned are indeed benefited. But when those energies move through an individual human, there are more resonances that are possible.

You are one human. You are a part of the community where you live. You are part of the whole of your country. You are part of the whole of all your geographical neighbors, and you are part of the world as a whole. It does not stop there, and that is our point. To be open, to recognize that you are not singular—not you in your own being, and not you in your own planet and species—that you are part of the whole multiverse, which includes so many systems, so many forms of being, so many frequencies of exchange. Opening to change, opening to accepting others, all of this is part of the path forward for individuals and for all.

For us, we have seen the path of ascension energies in our own histories. It is a long process, but your species and your planet, though young, have already been through a long process of developing and now it is time to support the changes that will heal the Earth and humanity so that they can continue to support each other in their evolving to ever higher vibrations of being.

The gift of the body

When you feel that you are alone, we want you to remember that you are not. You are connected. Every time you speak, every time you think a thought, every time you take any small action, you are moving in connection with the world around you. Your awareness of those connections may be weak or non-existent, but nevertheless you are surrounded. So one small step that you can take is to begin asking, 'What am I feeling around me? What am I sensing around me?'

We know there are many, many questions you could ask about what you are feeling inside you. But we are inviting you to be aware of what is around you when you just close your eyes quietly. It may be that you are simply feeling the warmth of the air, the heat of the sun, the chill of the air, the cold. Those are sensations that come from the physical world. And it is a joy, when you have a body, to feel those physical sensations. When you are feeling those sensations, it would be good to remember that when you do not have a body, there are no sensations like those that you feel now.

You see, you smell, you taste, you hear, you feel. Wherever you are, there are sensations that your skin picks up. There is sensation all around you. You open your eyes, you see color, you see shapes, you see forms. You close your eyes, you hear the birds. You hear footsteps in dried leaves. You hear rustling in trees. You hear a crack in the distance. You are a being of sensation.

It is one of the gifts of being alive on this planet, all these sensations that your body constantly has around it.

We would say that it is very important that you acknowledge the gift of these sensations. And yes, we know that some of what you sense you categorize as unpleasant. 'It is too cold. It does not feel good. It is too hot. The stones are sharp. They do not feel good on the feet.' Many sensations are not pleasant to you. And yet they are a part of the vibrancy of your life. When something is sharp and it cuts you, your nerves take that message to your brain. Imagine that there are people who do not have the ability to feel that. The absence of any of your senses creates dangers, stress, difficulties. When you can feel all those things, you are being given a gift.

And so we are saying, even those of you who are questing to be with spirit and the highest vibration, begin by being grateful for this incredible gift of the senses that being embodied here offers. Do not think of it as lesser. Lessons are gifted to you through your sensations. Yes, there are many ways to go astray with sensations. We absolutely understand this, but the foundation is to see sensation as a gift. And as with all gifts, to be grateful and to use the gifts wisely to acquire wisdom.

The first wisdom is to be grateful for the opportunity to feel, at the physical level, the sensations that are offered in embodiment. It is easy to think that this is lesser and that the higher vibration and frequency of spirit is better. But remember, that is not how your soul thinks. For the soul, the rich learning offered by those sensations is very powerful. So, just as you ground through your feet, we want you to ground yourself in gratitude for all the senses that you have available to you.

Changes to the human body

We want to discuss and explain the changes that occur in a physical body when the shift is made to a new plane of existence, in this case to a fifth dimensional plane. The human body is attuned and set to carry a field of very dense energies. The physical boundary of the body functions to some degree as a conscious barrier. While vibrations from the outside do penetrate to some degree, for the most part human awareness of their being stops at their external skin. At higher dimensions, the physicalized form becomes increasingly light, increasingly less dense. It is not that it is transparent. You have materials that are light in weight but not see-through. That is the sense in which we mean this. The physical body vibrates at a higher frequency. This higher frequency of the body resonates with the higher vibrations of the outside field.

This does not mean that every human brought into expression when the ascension to higher vibrations has been largely completed will be fully realized in the new dimension. Rather, souls will have the opportunity to use embodiments in the higher dimension to learn even more about moving into higher vibrations and sustaining those vibrations. There are some who have not been on Earth for a while and their soul will bring in embodiments to experience the joy of creating with a fuller array of higher vibrations.

For those who are here now, there may already be experiences of changes. Those who are already immersed in working on ascension in partnership with the Earth will be most likely to encounter changing needs of the body. There are things to eat and drink on the Earth plane that are dense, and things that are lighter. There are ways of eating and drinking that are more connected to denser and lower vibration and things that are themselves higher in vibration and that can be consumed with a higher vibration. On the simplest level, eating anything with gratitude helps to lighten the body. You may assume that drugs of the mind-altering kind, such as marijuana and alcohol, are denser in their energy because of how they distort the body's functioning.

We understand that there are drugs that assist people in opening their awareness of an expanded field of being. We are not discounting these experiences. We are saying that as the ascension moves forward, your body will be sending you messages about changes in diet that it will be important for you to heed. We know that the physical experience of the senses is an important part of human life, but you have already had many of those sensory experiences and this is a time to seek out the higher vibrations of your being, where the senses that you are attuning to are outside your body.

This is not to say that as of tomorrow you should foreswear all your current habits and pleasures. The ascension is a process of change. We are letting you know that your awareness, your field of energies and your physical body are all in a process of transitioning. Transformation means change. Change always means something that was ceases to be, while something new emerges.

You have yearned for this transformation. Humanity has been destined for this transformation. We are here to assist you as you prepare your own way forward and in doing so assist all of humanity and the Earth. You have the whole world in your hands. The channel finds that amusing and didn't want to write it down but it came forward because that song carries an energy that is exactly right for this transformation. When it is sung with meaning and an open heart it feeds the ascension energies. Sometimes the small things can carry untold and unseen power.

There is a speeding up now

There is a speeding up now that is occurring. This means that it is even more important that those who are able to bring their energy to a higher vibration do so as much as possible. It is at this moment that every addition to the energies that are accumulating carries even more impact. We do not like this word 'impact.' You do not have the words that speak to the rising of ever lighter form. We would like all who are awake to the light within to spend more time in a higher, lighter vibration so that it begins to take even deeper root, so that all your cells are attuned to this different energy.

What we are recommending is to sit in that energy of light, let that energy move throughout the physical form and throughout the field. It is not that the body is one thing and the energy field is another. They are one thing. And so there is the interpenetration of energies between this solidified form and what you are calling the etheric form. You make a distinction and yet it is all one. Manifesting differently, but all one, just as parts of the physical form make one body. Each aspect is manifesting differently but united in working as one thing, one being. Just so with the nonphysical aspect. It is simply another aspect of the being. We do not see physical form and nonphysical form. We see one being.

All who are awakened can seek practices that allow them to experience their nonphysical form and their physical form merged as one in their awareness. This is a practice that will benefit the energies that are now needed.

We also want you to be aware of those who bring forward sounds. Sounds can carry energies and are needed on your plane now. Though raising the vibration through the heart is a very important practice, open also to the possibility of sounds coming through that express and carry higher vibrations. There are those channels who can bring forward a language that is a form of translating the pure energies of other beings into a form that can be seen in movement and heard in sounds. It is not trying to bring forward words. It is bypassing words and just allowing the sounds. Some sounds are beneficial to the receiver's body. Other sounds are part of clearing. And yet other sounds carry the higher energies that are associated with the planet's healing and humanity's ascension and evolution.

Increase the vibration of love

There are many groups now that are beginning to focus on the idea of planetary ascension. This is a very large goal. The Earth is at once very far from this goal and at the same time poised to move toward it, taking what you would call a big step. But this step can only happen if the energies are there to support it. In order for there to be this step forward in the level of vibration, so that the effects of that higher frequency can be felt by all that is on the planet Earth, many, many smaller steps need to be taken first. Right now, the smaller step that is needed is the increase in the heart-centered flow, the vibration of what you call love.

There is much that distracts from the heart-centered vibration. When you watch the news, it evokes emotions, but it does not evoke love. When you are driving in your cars, many emotions are triggered, but rarely love. Even when you do your exercise in nature, riding your bicycle or taking your hikes or just taking a walk, there is not much love that is being put forth. Love is not a word. It is a vibration. Saying the word is not enough to evoke the vibration.

As you read or hear this message think about what evokes in you a strong feeling of unconditional love. A love that is not impeded by fear. Just a pure love. Sometimes this occurs with your animals, your pets. Sometimes this is evoked by another human. Sometimes it is evoked by beauty. Each of you need to identify, with great honesty, what pulls unconditional love from you. You all have this great capacity to love.

What is needed is for you to spend some time every day sending forth your feelings of love. Even if that love is going to your pet, the vibration is also released through your energetic field out into the energetic sphere surrounding the Earth. Whatever it is that calls forth your most generous love, you need to bring that forth every day. Just imagine if everyone in your world spent time every day focused on loving unconditionally and letting that vibration of unconditional love flow out from them. That loving vibration goes out into the atmosphere and it joins with all the other expressions that are at that same frequency, that same vibration in the energetic field of the Earth.

When you do any action with love, no matter what the action is, it is beneficial to the Earth. What you call love includes many different frequencies. Even love that is somewhat impeded, constrained, and limited, though not as high a vibration as unconditional love, is nevertheless a vibration that goes into the energetic atmosphere of the Earth, and is a help.

We see groups who choose to meditate together on planetary healing. When you focus your prayers on the Earth and all that lives upon it, that is very good. These acts are beneficial, but they are not enough.

It is important for you to know that you can make your own contribution every day, even if you spend only a few minutes on it, when there is a pause in your day. Your daily commitment to evoke unconditional love in yourself, so that it flows out and rises up and expands the frequency of unconditional love around the Earth, would be a blessing for the Earth. It would contribute to moving the Earth toward the possibility of ascension.

So that is the assignment we wish to put forward.

Co-creation is the future

When you are able to focus on the heart center of your body and the energy center around it, your heart chakra, you can begin to expand its area. As you intend to expand you will reach a point where your focus begins to resonate with your higher vibration of heart. This is what ascension is about—the resonances and waves of energies that are produced by each individual's own higher vibrations.

Many people feel that they need someone to do this for them and indeed there are teachers in body and spirit who assist people in feeling and experiencing their own higher energies. But in the next dimension of experience, the ability of a being to actualize these vibrations independently is central.

It is in a sense the individual's own activation of their higher energies that 'powers' the higher vibration of the dimension.

Now it is true that the planet emanates energies that support and nourish higher vibrations, but the Earth and embodied humans are in a close partnership. It takes both parts of the equation to maintain the higher energies of a higher dimensional plane. The Earth's energies are pushing against the past accumulation of denser energies. The rising higher vibrations are being fueled by the Earth's own mission and the higher vibrations added by humans into the field. But even as your own yearnings and desire for love, kindness, compassion, and light drive you to seek guidance, to meditate, to seek out others who wish and yearn for and seek the same, so do the Earth's drives grow stronger in pushing to be free of darker and denser energies, to have the expansion of creation in partnership with humanity.

As you seek to be more fully in your heart, the changes you undergo may include some loss. Those who cannot resonate with your higher vibrations may want to hold you back. They may drift or turn away; or you may turn away from them as you seek the light rather than the duller, denser vibrations of those who remain closed off. These changes can be painful, even as they bring more lightness to your being and to the energies around you.

So too, the Earth's movement toward higher vibrations will be manifested in physical changes. Understand these as part of the process of transformation and hold on to the vision of the future in which the Earth and humanity share a new freedom of being and a deeper, more rewarding partnership in their co-creations. For co-creation is the future of this world and those who inhabit it.

Just as you were always meant to grow up into ever fuller becoming, so too your species and your planet have always had ascension from this third dimension as part of the plan. Everything has been simply a step toward these moments of transformation and ascendence.

You have rituals in your world to mark completion of one stage and readiness for moving to the next one as you develop. This is such a time for the Earth and humanity. The date has not been set, but everything is being assembled in readiness. These are important days, months, years—the specifics do not matter, what matters is that the potential pathways now are mere variations. Ascension is moving forward, it is allowed. It will happen.

It is very important that you understand that you are a part of the momentum that is charged with carrying the ascension energies forward. Turn toward the light. That is a mission of your soul. It is the destiny of all the beings who are linked to the human template.

Share the light you hold

We call upon all those who know that they carry light within to increase their own light and to share this light. This is the light of the higher heart, of the greater Self. When you choose to open to your Higher Self, your greater Self, your connection to the Source of all creation, to that creation energy in yourself, when you are both connecting to the Earth and connecting to those Higher Self energies, then you bring to the Earth that which the Earth needs. You bring to all beings that which is needed.

What is important now is the changing structure, the changing amount of high light-filled energies going into the Earth, going out and across the entire planet, across the whole connective tissue of humanity. It is necessary, if you are aware of the light that is within you, that you hold that awareness every day for as much of the time as you can; that you intend to strengthen that light. Intend to send that light down into the Earth light grid. Intend to send out in connection to all others the energy of light that you hold, that you channel, that you give forth. That network of light across humans, connecting humans, that light from all those humans connecting down into the Earth, this is what creates the ascension to the next dimension.

This is why you are here at this time, with the awareness that you have. It is not that your everyday lives do not matter—that your other purposes, connected with the more mundane world and the learnings of your own being, do not matter. Of course they do. But at this moment an important role and purpose, an important service that you are here to be part of is to be in that light. Consciously. With awareness. To let that light move down into the Earth. Up into the heavens. Out across to all humans. Not by what you are doing, but by what you are intending. By what you are aware of. By what you choose.

And so that is our reminder always. Be aware of your light. Choose to hold your light. Choose to send that light to the Earth, and to all connections across humanity, that there may be this ascension to the next dimension. All of those who are present, gathered from many different systems outside of your plane and dimension, are here solely to assist you in this great moment of the Earth's evolution and humanity's expansion in consciousness.

This is a practice that can be experimented with—always putting forward the strongest intention to call in those energies that are available to be brought forward. By bringing them forward through your bodies and your voices, you amplify their integration into the field of the Earth.

The physical manifestation and transmission of energies is important. If we bring our energies and share them within the field of the Earth, they are received at a particular layer.

You could think of it as a plane of existence. To move the Earth and humankind forward, these vibrations must reach more layers, physical and nonphysical.

How does this happen? One way is through words. Even reading these words, which carry the energies we are sending forth through this transmission, is beneficial. It is also valuable to simply intend to transmit higher energies into the Earth's field, and into the matrix that connects with all the human species.

Use the power of your intention, your belief and your imagination to send out energies that will benefit the expansion to a higher vibrational plane. This is important for you to do, and for you to transmit and share with others.

Connect to your higher heart

There is one message above all others that it is important for you to hear. That is the message of your heart. Not the smaller heart that has its human loves and wounds and desires. But your own Higher Heart, that place of unconditional love that is a part of you and is your true home. Unconditional love is not something that you can only occasionally visit. Unconditional love is your soul's state of being, which exists in you. It is the highest vibration of love, of the highest heart energies fully opened.

Unconditional love is a place of presence. It is that place of knowing that All That Is, simply is. You are. It is powerful to be in that state of presence, that state of 'I am.' Here you have only love, kindness, compassion for self, for others. And it is not difficult. When you allow yourself to come home to your Higher Heart you rest in that unconditional love and acceptance and connection to all.

There is much, much in your world that pulls you away from your own state of unconditional love. You find in your lower self, in your third-dimensional awareness, that constant love, kindness, compassion, acceptance and presence are difficult. Very difficult. But remember that unconditional love is not outside of you. It is not something you have to earn. It is not something you can lose. It is at the core of your being. You can choose to open more and more to this part of yourself.

We ask that you choose to connect to your Higher Heart, to be in that place of unconditional love, in that essence of you. When you are connected to your Higher Heart, to that place that *is* you, love, kindness and compassion are present to whatever is occurring. When you connect to your Higher Heart, you raise your vibration and expand the light for your being and for all beings.

The times that are here and the times that are coming will challenge you. But the answer to the challenge is for you to remember who you are. You are that greater Self. Your truth is in your Higher Heart. Your truth is in your unconditional love, presence, kindness and compassion.

There are many here with you supporting the changes in consciousness and expanding light of the Higher Heart energies as your planet and humanity moves toward ascending to a higher dimension. We are honored to be with you on this journey.

Expand your compassion

We are watching the reactions to all that is happening, not just in your country or place of being, but around this entire Earth. And there are pockets, places where calm is being held and where there is a heartbeat of compassion and caring. But even that is being disrupted because of all that is happening on so many layers, particularly the disruptions the Earth is going through. There may be compassion for victims of natural disasters, but that is not the energy of compassion that is most beneficial. That is a reaction to a loss, to something that was painful, which engages suffering and empathy for those who are bewildered.

The compassion that is beneficial at the moment is a higher vibration. It is larger vibration in the sense that it carries further, has more energy in it. It is a compassion that is separate from events. Yes, you feel sorry for those who are caught in the flood and lose their homes. You feel badly for the town, the city, the area that has suffered losses. In this, you are reacting to an event, which elicits your sympathy, your empathy, and even a sense of compassion. But because it is evoked by an event, it is... smaller. It is not compassion for the whole. That understanding and level of compassion is difficult for many of you to grasp. Part of understanding and accepting where the world is going means understanding that there will be losses and changes as the world moves toward a new place of being.

We want you to consider holding a compassion for humanity as a whole, not individuals affected by certain events, to whom you direct your compassion, but compassion for the whole of your species, the whole of humanity. The whole of the Earth. And also the whole of your own being.

You may think that compassion for the self is the smallest, but it is not. We want you to seek from within yourself compassion for the whole of you, not just in relation to events or losses that were painful. We speak of compassion for the entirety of the journey. This is difficult to achieve because of the density of this plane and because of what the soul has asked to learn in this lifetime. There have been challenges. And there has been excitement and joy. And so, when you hold compassion for the Self that continued through, that compassion has a sense of wonder, yes? It does not hold pain. That vibration of compassion is a vibration of holding hope, and even joy.

This is difficult to communicate because of how your words are fixed and used. We do not use your vocabulary and are not limited to associations with your connotations, denotations, all those things that attach to your words and their use. We communicate through energies, through vibrations and so there are different notes, different vibrations. Often what you are calling compassion is not of the vibration that we are wanting to bring forward here.

As the transition of the Earth and humanity unfolds, it will be beneficial for you to hold your whole being in joy and in the compassion. You are a being who is going through life experiences and learning of all kinds. Let your compassion for your being hold your courage.

You see, we are not saying pride. We are not saying pride in the Self. We are saying compassion for the Self. That is a different energy. That compassion holds, as we say, an energy of deep hope and joy in possibilities and potentials. It supports getting back up and trying again. It is a compassion that lifts up. You are not joining in sadness. You are not reacting. You are sustaining a positive place where you hold compassion for the whole.

Practice with the Self. Practice holding your entire Self, all that you have experienced and been through, in the arms of your compassion, by which we mean, in the energy of hope, the energy of accepting the whole of you without judgment.

What is the difference between unconditional love and what we are calling compassion? Well, you could call it unconditional compassion. It is not conditioned by an event, by a sadness. It arises in accepting, allowing, holding the whole of what is. The compassion that we are speaking of is an energy of embracing and allowing without conditions or judgments. Unconditional love is also a state of being apart from any judgments. Unconditional love is a state of being that radiates a very high vibration wave that nourishes and opens. It is possible to receive and send forth this energy.

So we are trying to suggest the importance of expanding your understanding of these words. We encourage you to let go of how you have had these words defined and limited in the past. Instead of fixing on the words and their past meaning and use, open to the expanded meaning and the difference in vibration. This type of attunement is part of the changes that are coming, where there is less reaction and more connection to what endures, to what is thought of as the All.

Working with energies is important to move things forward for humanity and always it is important to start with the Self. Start with the Self, hold your whole being in compassion, in that sense of deep hope and joy in all that you as a human being can experience and learn. Hold this as an intention with your heart, and support will be present.

Connect with others

This is a time when the accumulated energies moving toward the ascension of the planet and humankind are gathering with ever greater force. This means that there are more and more beings who are seeking to express and generate love, kindness, and generosity of the highest order; more and more beings who are recognizing that they hold the light within them and that no matter what darkness surrounds them, they can lift up their own light. But this is also a time when the lifting up of individual lights, the individual recognition of the light that you have within you, is not sufficient to bring forward the ascension.

What is needed now is for each of you who knows that you are carrying the light of consciousness, the higher vibration of love, the ability to recognize the power of Divine source creation energies—it is time for you to link with others. There are many ways to do this. There are those who are channeling messages and channeling meditations, which you can follow, listen to, participate in. When you do this at the same time as others, it unites the energies, resulting in what your mathematicians call an exponential effect. The ascension energies need that exponential push, that exponential increase.

On the planet and among humankind right now, there are great expressions of darkness, great disruptions. There is war, there are massacres, there are raging, raging angers. There are great sorrows. There are great losses. There is much that holds the darker energies. Those of you who know your connection to the light, who know your connection to your heart energies, who can sense your expansion and connection to spirit—it is for you to avoid being drawn to the darkness but instead to join together with others who are conscious of the light.

It is time to push. In your birthing process there is a time when you must push so that the birth can be realized. For the ascension to be realized you must join together, breathe together and push out the light.

Expand the light. Remember and call forth the light and the higher vibration of love to which you are connected, which are a part of you—not expecting that the world will be healed, but knowing that the world is changing and will emerge newborn, and that humankind will emerge as a species into a new potential of being.

This is important work that you are here to do. Whatever you are doing in your life that keeps you living and safe is all very well and good, but you are here to be part of the birth of the new Earth and the new human species. That is what the ascension is about. It is an evolution to the new. No calling is more sacred in your terms.

We ask you to allow the pain that will be part of the birthing process, while you focus your heart, your love and your joy on what will be arising.

We are here because we honor this process, which we know from our own histories of long, long ago. We honor you who are holding the light and making this ascension possible. Without you it cannot occur.

TEACHINGS FROM ANDRAUS AND THE LIGHT COLLECTIVE

ANDRAUS' INTRODUCTION TO THE TEACHINGS

I t is with great delight that we, Andraus and the Light Collective, bring this work to you now because it is a time of great transition and we want you to understand the way forward. This work is a pathway for you to practice and to participate in. Please read the whole material to understand the process and the way forward and then on the final page, there is a transcript of the meditation or pathway for you to work through on a regular or daily basis. It is this work that we ask you to commit to doing regularly.

You will find in the introduction a section where Laura talks about her experience of this pathway and this meditation, but of course it is and will be different for each of you and therefore I and the Light Collective bring you our blessings and our support directly when you work with this material. It is not a simple process; it will take you into many nooks and crannies. We will be with you and we will guide you directly if you call upon us. This is our contribution to your evolution and we will be blessed to do so.

These messages are for everybody who resonates and has an interest in them. We have tried to keep them as simple as possible because for many who resonate, there will have been many years of spiritual practice. We are not trying to overlay a new spiritual practice on you, but simply to encourage you to see the way forward as a whole.

Many people will now be coming to this for the first time and to these people we say "welcome." For others it has been a practice of many years, if not a lifetime, and so the work for you is to recalibrate for the new realm that is coming upon us and is here now. We will expand on this in more detail in the coming sessions. I hope this work will be of use to you.

For those who find these words and messages helpful, there will be a passage through for everyone who takes part in the process of reading or disseminating the material. And that is our aim, simply to give a pathway for as many as are interested in finding their way along and through this time of transition.

I. THE GREAT TRANSITION: AWAKENING TO THE CALL OF YOUR SOUL

Understanding the transition

There are many challenges and difficulties ahead. There will be conflict, upheaval, enormous challenge to the societal order and to the current way of being in this world. The status quo will be shaken to its roots. The institutions that have served well up until this time will be in disarray. In this challenging time, there is an energetic opportunity to hold firm, to be seen in your own authenticity as you withstand the loss of these structures.

If you are aware, attuned and expecting this to take place, you can maintain your alignment with your own understanding of the situation, rather than tuning in to the general panic and disarray that many will find themselves in. It is the societal norm to look at the negative, rather than the positive, so what I would like to do is to re-educate your mindset and state of being so that you are able to simply allow the destruction of the temple.

There will be a period of mourning, distress and dissolution, while others come to terms with what they will see as a disaster. Then there will come a new awakening, a new way of being and a new energetic structure which will encompass the thoughts of those who are willing to enquire, reach out, enable, and encourage the places within that are knowledge-able about this situation and are willing to be vulnerable to a new way of being, a new way of life, and a new way of under-standing the world.

This will obviously be a difficult transition for many, but it is the seeds of a new beginning for a new society that will flourish, because there has been a break with the continuity of past and present. If there is more understanding of this at the outset, it will be a smoother transition for many, so it is our task and our pleasure to bring this work through now to enlighten as many as possible before the events unfold.

Connect to your soul

There is a great light in the darkness at this time: and this is your connection to your own soul. Your heart and soul are very much attuned to the transition that is taking place. When you are ready, you will find new openings. So do not be attuned to the news, to talk of disaster, but attune yourself to the places within that are opening up. The energy is so great now and there is such opening. As structures begin to disintegrate, you will begin to sense new ways of being, and to move toward the way forward for your soul's journey.

It is important that you pray every day, taking time to contemplate and connect with your soul's purpose in this life. You will be guided forward by the internal light, warmth and strength that will come through from your soul's purpose. Your soul's connection to your conscious way of being will then drive you forward, not with fear and hesitation, but with an openness to yourself and a kindness to others. Then you will see that there is no need to worry about the future of mankind, because it is simply a new direction and an increased awareness of each other that will develop in the coming times.

We would very much like to offer a way of hope and a new glimpse at the paradigm that is coming upon us now, which will drive the next human evolutionary cycle. It is something to embrace because it brings about a whole new set of opportunities and exciting possibilities.

Recently there have been great ruptures of the traditional structures that have held communities and societies together. There are places in the world that are beginning to disintegrate through war, trade wars or in terms of their management structures. The rule of law is perhaps not as constant as it might have been in the past.

What is important about this time is that there is the opportunity for change, growth and evolution. There is a path through the apparent destruction of what once was held up as ideal. In the present time there are new openings for people to begin to question: "Well, what is my thought process about this? What do I believe? What are my priorities here? What is important to me? Where am I going with this type of change? How do I wish to change and what are the first steps to embrace this change?" It is important to see that there is no preset structure to the newness of these aspirations.

It is time to reach out and perceive that there many others who are beginning to question: "What's next? What's coming into being? What is this cultural (r)evolution? How can we progress as a community, as a nation, as a species?" It is important to begin this process of thinking, of deliberating. Nothing needs to be done immediately because there is still a dissolution process to go through. As things begin to dissolve, there will be more time and space for new perspectives to arise. This comes not from an intellectual thought process, but from within and around: from cultural dissolution that dissipates some of the norms. As this happens, people begin to think: "Well, what's left? What's next?"

In this transitional state, it is important to begin to think positively about what is happening, because if the negative begins to take hold, then the positive becomes more difficult to achieve. So therefore, I would caution, warn and indeed emphasize that it is the positive nature of this change that must be focused on, taking away the need to worry and the desire to protect one's own patch. If you can open to the positive, and hold that, then that is what can be created because it is thought and intention that creates, on Earth and in the universe.

Begin the work now

It is important to begin to work now with other like-minded souls who are working with this process to create a positive, creative new evolutionary culture at this time. This is a very important moment in human evolution because it begins a new stage of human development. There are many spirit guides here to support this change, this movement, and we would like to help and support you, and to hold a healing space for you to move past any fears and holding patterns and move into a much more positive and productive state of mind.

This means that you will need to let go of old structures, old patterns and old ways of thinking of things and seeing the world, keeping a positive and inquiring mindset in the face of dissolving boundaries and new emergences.

Do not be afraid of this time. Do not be alarmed at the actions of others who seem to be taking advantage of the situation. That is not your concern. What is important in this time is to bring forward new energies, to step forward with a workmanlike rolling-up-of-sleeves to say "Right, I am here. I have come to assist with the evolutionary movement forward of my species. I do not want to wait and take part in the negative cycle of destruction. I want to bring forward a new evolutionary way of thinking about life."

So that is why I am speaking to you now, because I would like to motivate and encourage you to come on board with us on this journey. We can help you begin to see what the next steps are and how to achieve them.

The energies of the present time

There is a great deal of suffering in your world at this time, and we are sorry that this is the case, but there is a channel that can be utilized to bring more positive dealings with the spirit world into being. At this time, there is a lot of savory (positive) and unsavory (negative) energy. Both are present, both are available, and it will benefit you to choose savory over unsavory energy.

It is important to be aware that there are a great number of sources of positive material. It is not just our channeled work here that will help you with this decision-making process. Many spirit beings are working to bring this work forward now.

There is a changing understanding of spirituality and the importance of one's spiritual journey. it is not enough for people to think: "I can do that in my spare time or when I retire." spiritual awareness must be always integrated into one's life. This has always been the case, of course, but now more than ever it is very important that everybody be aware that their spiritual life matters. It is part of who you are and what you have to bring to the world, but it is also how the world evolves.

So part of the attuning process, the re-tuning process, is undoing the restraints and the disbelief that leads to an absence of spirituality, and bringing a belief in spiritual growth into the workspace, the social space and the family space. Everybody has a spiritual life because it is part of your energetic makeup, and it is very important currently that everybody understands that this is an extension of who you are.

This represents an evolution and expansion of who you believe yourself to be. Human beings are not just physical beings. You are not just molecules; you are also energy and spirit. All of these elements come together to make you both human and spirit—not just physical, but also alive with the spirit that makes you who you are.

The call to action

Your spirit is always attuned to the Divine and to the larger context, and it is your spiritual self that is coming forward now. This is why we are here: to bring this call to action through more forcefully, in a way that helps you experience your spiritual lives more fully, more completely integrated into your day-to-day existence.

How does that begin to happen? You might well see that it is already underway, but perhaps you have not yet noticed. Have you noticed your breath on a cold day—how sometimes you can see it, and sometimes you cannot. This is perhaps how you might feel when you notice that your life is not just physical. You begin to think: "What else is here now?

What is my purpose? What is the point of my life?" With this inquiry, the spirit is freed again to bring more life into being. But it is important to see that the spirit is not simply individual. It is part of the collective spirituality of your species, and therefore it is important to be aware that you are part of a larger whole when you live from spirit.

So it is with great delight that I say, 'Come with us on this journey of the spirit. Bring your friends, bring your family, bring your children and see that spirit lives.'

How to experience spirit

Let us say that you wish to experience spirit. How is this done? It is done through the simple process of stopping, listening to what is going on with your body and being still for some time. Take 15 minutes and sit. Light a candle and think: "What is this light about? Where within me do I find the light shining brightly?" In truth, it is in every cell of your body.

It is with great delight that I say that you have this light within you, as each person who has been born into the human form has this light within them in every cell of their being. This is what I am trying to attract your attention to. There is light within you, light around you, light in every person that you meet. Begin to ask yourself: "How do I experience that light?"

11. ENTERING THE PATHWAY OF SPIRITUAL EVOLUTION

Transition and the tapping

Your energy system is evolving, leading to a change in the energetic vibration around you. This is creating a new system for people to be able to work more deeply in their own lives. Not by looking inward so much but by sharing what is happening, by opening to consider other ways of being, other ways of thinking, other ways of opening one's own heart and soul to the possibility that there is a spiritual life.

There is a spiritual reality that is extending itself into your life. It is tapping you on your shoulder and saying: "What is going on here? What is happening in the world? What is it that I am meant to take from this?" This tapping will become more regular and more urgent, because for everybody there is a sense of "What is going on? What is happening?" These are important questions.

The way to work with these new questions is to say to yourself: "I would like to participate in this new energy. I would like to grab the reins and welcome this new energy. I am seeking, inquiring, asking for guidance, asking the spirits to come to me and bring me to a new place of reality, to open me, to work with me, to shape me into something new, to offer me something that will resonate within me so I can say,

'Yes, this is my way forward. This is what I want to do with my life, this is where I am going. These are the new sensations that are changing me, evolving me, moving me forward and helping me to understand what this next stage of my life and the life of others is about.'"

There are great issues arising in your social and economic situation, but the opportunity is to distance yourself from the sense of crisis management. Instead, begin to ask: "What is going to change? What needs to change? How do I move forward? There is an inevitable cracking, a breaking apart, but in that breaking apart something new is evolving and that is where my sight line is; that is where my energy is; that is how my value system is changing to adapt to new realities."

You may find yourself at a place of beginning, opening and reaching toward a new destination. There is a current carrying along those who wish to participate. It is a choice and a participation that comes by thinking: "I am not going to get involved in the negativity here. I am going to move with the positive current that takes me in a new direction, and while I don't know where I'm going, I trust that the new direction is positive and is evolving my being and my psyche, as I contact and connect in new ways with the greater aspect of life."

Transition and the collective

It is a time of change and transition, but also a time of hope. There is an opportunity for the human species to evolve, to move past its limitations and its idealistic sense of its own importance—to move toward a new collective way of being in and seeing the world, a new way of participating in the world that will break through the negativity of the past human individualistic relationship to the world and its resources.

The old ways are no longer working for humanity and for planet Earth. It is time to move past this into a new collective awakening, a time of transition that will bring a better sense of one's collective responsibility to the world. This is a beautiful time of transition because for those who embrace the new energy, there is an opportunity to say: "Wait a minute, there is something new here."

In the energy that is awakening, there is a pulse. There is a life form. There is a sense of collective responsibility, a sense of coming together with others in a way that has not really been experienced in the past. This new sense of collective responsibility will be shared worldwide and is not something where you say: "I am Chinese," "I am Asian," "I am Western." These designations will no longer matter. What is coming into being is a new collective human species which can communicate to all corners of the globe, at a much higher resonance, with no need for these terms of the past.

It is important to begin to understand that there is no longer a need for boundaries and resource guarding. There is now a need for a communication that expands beyond intense defensive structures. For many millennia, humans have lived defensively, which has brought a sense of closure: the sense that there must be a structure, a boundary, a definition of what is one's own particular resource. But this is no longer appropriate, because this communication goes beyond the need for physical or personal definition.

What is needed now, and what is coming through in the energetic wave of (r)evolution, is that you expand beyond the limited individualistic definition to find common ground. You will find ways of participating in something larger, going beyond those limited old boundaries and definitions. This is new energy that is coming now. It is already here, to be honest, but it is evolving, it is developing, and it is bringing you with it.

Consider—are you already beginning to perceive something new that is tapping on your shoulder? Are you willing to stay with these words and with this work until you can see where they might have a resonance for you?

Transition and your spiritual life— what's here now?

During this difficult time of transition, with many searching questions arising from the lack of coherent structure, you are very much in a time of change and evolution. There is a lot of work to be done around the edges of your evolutionary experience and journey, and I am pleased to be a guide on that path for you.

We have been doing this work with humanity, with other species and with other worlds for many millennia. There are always a few bumps on the road, but it is a tried and proven method to begin to move into the higher realms of your own spiritual being.

We are all spiritual beings. We are all of spirit. We all have a spiritual life and a spiritual existence, and we are all in this together. While we may not be on Earth with you in a human body, we are also of spirit, as are you. Your soul has incarnated in this time to help you understand the evolutionary process. It has its difficulties, but it will help you grow in the long term, and that's what is essential at this time. So, put one foot forward at a time. The next step in your process is to think: "Well, what now? What is here now?"

Sitting in the "what's here now?" will help you to move forward. What's here now? Sitting with curiosity, not with judgment, not with action, not with any distractions, but simply noticing what's here now. What's here now within you and around you? What's here now in terms of your physical body, your sense of energetic aliveness, your emotional and mental states? What's here now? And then having compassion for what comes through. It is not something that needs to be judged, removed or changed. It is simply noticing what's here now. That is where we begin: with the words: "What's here now?"

Transition and questioning

Currently there is a void and emptiness, and everybody currently feels this sense of questioning: "What's next? What is coming through?" What is required at the present time is simply to sit with these questions. It is another day of great pain in the world, unfortunately. There are many events taking place on Earth which are not in alignment with the overall universal template. When we are in line and in tune with the universal template, an energy comes upon us which is much closer to the truth. There is no conflict with any other soul, and there is indeed a unification process, which brings together the energy fields of many souls to work together.

The Light Collective is one example of that. It is a universal gathering of souls and spirit beings who wish the same outcome or purpose: the healing of those upon the planet who want to see a clearer route to the Divine matrix that governs the universe. When one tunes into that intention and asks for that unification process to be engaged, a clarity comes through.

The unification process occurs when one is in tune, aligned, and in harmony with that process, understanding and perhaps asking for help for the alignment to take place. Your own guides and spirit beings are around you to help you to reimagine, remember and re-align with that place in your own life. This is a process of moving into alignment with the Divine as an energetic imprint, which is the template of your body and soul and All That Is. There is always a place within you that seeks the Divine. That is your spiritual quest and your spiritual purpose. Sometimes it is blocked in a given lifetime because it has not been clarified to you that this is important.

Others might say that there is no purpose to life, there is nothing beyond this life. This is a blockage, and it comes with a lot of pain and misunderstanding, with a sense of frustration that others are blocking one's light. It is important to reimagine this frustration as a question, a tapping on the shoulder that asks: "What is going on here? What is this frustration? What is this discomfort I am feeling?"

It is so important for you all to become aware of this tapping and this questioning. It happens to all of you, and all of you need to listen because it is pointing toward the higher way forward. It leads to the ultimate question, to the experience of God or the Divine. A lot of human endeavor has been taken up by the Divine quest and now it is time to recognize the existence of a greater quest, a greater alignment. This is required now for all humanity in this planetary time because the alignment has slipped or become weaker than in past ages. Now is the time for the spiritual quest to become a very important question in everybody's life. How people choose to address this question is of importance. There must be avenues and ways for people to think: "Oh, I know what is happening now. I understand what that question is saying to me. I have some outlets and some avenues to explore. I understand what the first footstep forward on the path might be."

It is a time of exciting change because that question, "What is going on here?" is of paramount importance and must be listened to and explored.

Transition and the spiritual realm

There are many who do not understand the magnitude of this change and new growth in the human evolutionary cycle. We would like to bring forth information that will help you begin to unfold and embrace the new way of being. There will be a period of disruption, but the guidance that we would give in this moment is simply to lean into the spiritual realm and ask for the assistance of your guides and spiritual companions. They will give you a new way of tackling the current moment.

In effect, it is saying to the spiritual realm: "I am aware that you exist, and I would like you to help me." What would happen if you did this? You would reach into the ether and ask for Divine assistance, for your spirit guides to surround you and to give you assistance. In doing this, it is important to be aligned with the higher, most Divine powers who are in accord with your best interests. Align with the Divine higher energies who will give you a sense of comfort and bathe you with their particular essence, allowing you to perceive that there is a being who is with you in spirit.

It may be difficult to imagine this, as it is not something that is easy to discern, and for many it might seem a little fanciful. But believe me, we are here; we care about your spiritual development and evolution, and we wish to assist you. It would be a benefit to you to reach out and say: "I would like guidance; I would like you to surround me with your wisdom and light at this time." You may be surprised at the outcome and what comes into your awareness, and you will be off on a new adventure with your spirit guides, your spirit team. It is time for everyone to be reaching into this realm, so that we can assist you with this shift. Reaching outwards and upwards in the spiritual realm will assist you with your transition.

How is this accomplished? By sitting in contemplation, in quiet, in solitude and asking for assistance; by setting your intention to contact your guides and for them to respond in whatever way is appropriate and will be meaningful for you. This is a time of renewal for the human spirit because for some millennia it has been a rather fanciful and a neglected part of the human condition. In fact, it is an important and essential part of the new way of being in the world. Everyone has a spiritual dimension to them that is available to connect with. It is an exciting time, and I hope you will join us in this endeavor.

Transition and spiritual community

There is a lot of new energy coming through currently. It is of benefit to all who are interested and can sit to receive the energy available. I am not saying that this is a time of great healing, transformation, or transition, but it is a preparation for the work at hand. So, it is time for everyone to focus, listen and to be of good cheer, knowing that there is a new way of being coming into existence and that all who are interested and feel called to do so can open themselves to this new energy.

It takes a little imagination and faith to open to this new realm and to understand that traditional religious and faith realms are having to adapt to new ways of being, which is why churches and other places of worship are not full of younger souls currently. The older souls are perhaps inured to the changes that are taking place within the spiritual realm, but this will not stop the expansion of all spiritual and religious faiths because it will become apparent to others that there is a new and more powerful energy coming through that will help to develop the Christian and other spiritual and religious faiths in ways that will make them adaptable to today's requirements.

I would like to emphasize that there is strength in numbers. There is strength in being part of a faith community that is embracing the existence of a spiritual dimension because this gives more energy to the possibility that this new life will come through. It is important to be part of a local faith community. One must feed the communities around you with the faith background that you have and give to others as they give to you.

It is not enough to try to do this alone, because others need to understand and be with the type of change that is coming into place. So, I encourage you all to find a place to explore your spiritual quest, whether it be a meditation group, or a spirituality group or a traditional faith group. The energies that are coming through are not particular to one group or another. They are coming through to all and it is of great benefit to you to join with others in taking in this new energetic reality. In the coming years, it is spiritual reality that will give you the most satisfaction, providing you with a solid and supportive base for your evolution.

Transition and beginnings

There are a lot of other beings who are here to assist the human evolution into a new spiritual dimension and there are a lot of messages like mine emanating around the globe, coming from different speakers, but all saying essentially the same thing, which is that there is now a new evolution of humanity underway.

It is in the interest of humanity to understand the process and to be situated within the field of light, evolution, and transition. This takes place simply by being attuned to one's own spiritual being and raising one's own energetic field and energetic radiance so that it becomes apparent that there is a new and further realm to discover and explore—the spiritual realm. This realm shows you the way forward, providing a marker for the spiritual being in the dimension of space and time. In the spiritual realm, time does not matter in the same linear way. In the progress of the individual and the collective evolutionary cycle, participation is more important than a timeline.

It is important to sit down every day and find a quiet space inside. Begin to focus and discern by a meditative practice that brings you deeper into your own energetic field. Be conscious of where you are in that energetic field. Then raise your vibration to a higher and stronger vibration that will begin to reach out into the next realms, where there is a spiritual sense, a spiritual purpose and a new way of thinking and perceiving the world.

All human beings have a spiritual life, a spiritual self, a part of the soul that is quite distinct from their physicality and is a connected way of being. All spiritually minded people know this at heart, but not always with consciousness. This spiritual dimension needs to be exercised and leaned into so that there can be a new, positive connection with one's spirit team and with the spiritual realm overall. This will give a sense of purpose, direction and commonality, because in the spiritual realm, all humanity lives in harmony and in collective unity.

In this realm, there is no war. There is no deficiency. There is no duality. A unitive and collective perspective is discerned from the connection with another in spirit form, and that connection will give a sense of community, hopefulness and evolution. It will provide the next steps on an individual and on a collective basis. Knowing what one's next steps are in this realm gives a sense of confidence—the sense that you know the next steps forward in your own life.

A new doorway for communication

You are being transformed by the energies around you. It is such a time of change that there is a tendency to see it as synonymous with the disruption and upset of world events, but it is not the same. The world's events might emerge from some of the energetic changes, but they are a by-product of the changes taking place. Look around you and understand that there are changes, schisms, reconditioning, realignment, relaxation and remembering of parts of the human psyche that have been lost in recent history.

There is a new value system emerging. It is a value system that promotes and encourages difference and new ways of living, working and being kind to each other. It is a system that promotes health, well-being and generational shifts toward new growth for the planet, with less waste. I know you can see all these things. These are the markers of good news and there is more good news to follow. In particular, the idea that we can communicate with each other mentally, not physically, will become important.

There are ways for us to communicate with you directly. To understand this, you need simply to sit back and ask for a conversation with spirit to be brought forward. With practice and foresight, a good connection can be made, and it can be quite simple to do this. It does not necessarily require many years of practice. An important step is to know that you are connected and that what is being said is not coming from you directly, but rather from spirit.

This is a place that has many pitfalls because there are other energies and blockages which will get in the way and bring forward perhaps a less accurate message. It is important simply to get out of the way and to allow the voice, the message, to come through by being attuned and letting the energetic interface interact with your voice and bring forth a new set of messages. In this moment, for example, I am saying to Laura to step back and let me work through her without any great interference because it can be difficult to let go and simply let the words pour through.

It is with this in mind that I say that you can do this most succinctly by being present with your own energetic field and letting your mind wander to the purpose of your contemplation. What is it that you wish to know? What is it that you wish to have clarified? In reaching out to one's guides and one's spiritual team, these questions can be answered for you, at least in part.

Be mindful and give thanks for the blessings that are around you, whether it be a spouse, a nice place to live, a new item of clothing or perhaps a child or an animal or a relative or friend who has come to visit. All these things are blessings, and they should be celebrated. When you understand that you are the very epitome of a blessed being, this gives you the energetic courage to reach out further and to assist others. "Look! I am very much attuned to the energetic reality of where we are currently. I understand what is going on, what is taking place, the changes that are coming about and I have confidence in the accuracy of my knowledge."

It is not something to hide. Change is happening, and it must be embraced by everybody. Things will not be the same. Feelings will not remain constant. Issues will be emerging, changing and breaking apart and there will be deaths, losses and new beginnings. That is the time in which you are living.

There is a new doorway through which to step and give thanks for the new beginnings that are coming if one follows this pathway. So, I would say to you: open the door, stand in the doorway and recognize that this is a good place to begin a new journey, to take a step forward into the future, which will be quite different from where humanity has been in the past millennia.

This has been foretold before, it is not new, but in the telling of it, it has been sanitized so that it has not been clear that humanity must pass through an unsettled time which will bring change by both negative and positive means. We are standing in the doorway to that time.

III. STRUCTURE FOR A DAILY PRACTICE OF LIGHT: GROUNDING, CONNECTION AND COMMUNION

The beginning of a new era

When this work is attended to, it brings the ability to switch into a higher vibration and a new beginning for everyone. You are moving into a new era of religion, spirituality and all faiths that take you in the same direction, which is to work together to increase the vibration amongst you so that the intensity of the vibration brings the energetic expansion needed.

It is hard to do this alone. It needs to be done in connection with others, whether this is family, friends, relatives or animals who can be aware of this change. Start with a friend, colleague or an individual who has similar interests to you, whom you can spend time with, so that there is a meeting of the minds that will allow new energies to come through.

It is a gift to be connected to another person or an animal in a way that can expand one's energy field to encompass the possibility of new growth, new development and a new way of communicating. One can say that this is a time of great division, yes, but it is also a time of coming together on a new level that does not need the healing of old divisions, because you are being moved forward in this respect.

I would ask you firstly to be in a pair or in a group and to ask another to be with you in spirit and to communicate with you in spirit. Reach out to them in spirit; reach out energetically without speaking or thinking, but with the heart, with the energy field, with the purpose of connecting and communicating in a different way, at a higher level, in a new sense. In your pair or group, sit in meditation and reach out to the other in silence and speak to them, not with your mouth, but energetically. Let them respond to you and see if you can have a conversation.

Afterwards, sit together and say, "Well, what did you experience? How did you experience that? What do you think we talked about?" Let that be a first experiment and see where things develop.

An energetic calling

There is a new way of being, a new energetic calling that invites perception by working beyond the mind, allowing oneself to reach out energetically and to say: "What is here now?" You will find that the heart and mind work together, and the body and mind work together. Working as one, the body and mind bring forward the transition that deepens the connection of body and soul with the heart. In that connection there is a new purpose. There is a new depth. There is excitement for the next stage of life. It is in this connection, in this meeting place, that the soul expands. In the practice of this expansion comes a new energetic light, framework and way of perceiving and distinguishing what comes next.

I would like you to sit and to bring forward the connection of spirit into your heart. Focus on the heart and intend that there be a meeting with the soul. What is the soul but an energetic place within the body where spirit, mind and soul connect? It is an exciting place. It is a place of passion, light, new galaxies and new energies that bring alive a new way of thinking and being in this world.

You are living in a formative time. Each one who brings forward and practices this heart connection brings a new light, a new way of being and a new connection with others. It takes practice. And so, I will now set out these steps of practice, to help you understand how the practice can come together in a way that brings new life.

Practice grounding every day

It is very important to be grounded every day. There are grounding exercises which can help you to remain in a more grounded and therefore more expanded state. Be aware that grounding is a very important aspect of staying balanced and remaining healthy.

Grounding also interrupts the tendency to over-think, over-analyze and worry. A grounding exercise every day will give you more flexibility in your life for creativity, balance and a healthy flow of the Earth's energies. Grounding will help you stay in balance in these changing times because it brings a certain calmness that it can be easy to forget in the moment.

Grounding means deepening into the Earth's energies by putting your feet on the ground and reaching deep into the Earth's core with your intention. Be open to the grounding energies coming through the feet, legs and body and bring this energy into each realm of your energy field.

This is a short process—it does not need to take more than 5 or 10 minutes. It is a very soothing, calming, and enriching process that will give you more and better stability in these changing times. Grounding is also important as it gives a foundation and base for the spiritual work that we do together.

Ground, breathe, and relax into the sense of being fully present on the Earth. Be aware that you are not separate from the Earth and that an energetic connection with the Earth gives you great pleasure. Be aware of this grounding right now.

You have a great medical dispensary at your disposal because you have the Earth's energy to plug into. Although there may be a lot of disturbance around you, the Earth's energy is stable and balanced. Nature is the place where you will find that balance: whether in the sea, sky or air, or in the forests, fields or gardens that you inhabit.

I would like you to spend time here: thinking of grounding into the sea, into gardens, into flowers, into trees, into the hills, into the rivers. Give yourself time to bathe in the natural flow of the Earth's energy—it will calm you. It will slow down your thinking and give you the sense of inner peace that begins to open you to the inner spiritual world. As you open to and become one with the inner spiritual world, you reach out to the spirit world around you and that gives more pleasure because you realize that you are not alone.

The pathway into the spiritual realm

You are not alone on this quest. Spirit is tapping on your shoulder. This is true for many others who are also seeking and moving in the same direction as you. You are beginning to see what is spinning around you. You are beginning to seek out other energetic beings and feel many energetic connections.

You are longing. You are reaching out. You are moving past yourself and your sense of limitation—and suddenly you are not alone. You are finding that because you are in a spiritual realm, there are many beings around you who are holding you up, encouraging you, welcoming you, and embracing you: who are very keen and excited that you have joined them.

That is what the spiritual journey is. This is the pathway to the next stage. It is not difficult or magical and it is very much a natural human and spiritual endeavor. It comes naturally to all human beings but is not taught in the human realm now in great depth or with regularity, as it should be. It has been taught in the past, but it has been forgotten in today's modern world of gadgets. So, it is a matter of remembering that this spiritual place is mundane and it is in every aspect of your life. It is not something that you need to go to a monastery or a retreat to experience as it is all around you and not something that you are alone in.

When you feel alone or when you feel that longing for connection: ground, reach in, feel the sense of longing and then reach out and you will find that there is a pathway. You will be drawn and guided to the next steps and how to reach where you should be. If you wish to find a new church or new spiritual group, this is the process to engage in because it will give you a direction for the journey. If you are feeling exhausted, lonely or depressed, this process will excite and engage you and make you feel alive and vibrant again.

We bring a joyful message. It is a message of excitement and enlivenment, and it is a way to connect the dots to discover the next aspects of your journey. Where is it that you wish to journey to? Where is it that you wish to take your life? Where is it that will bring you energetic joy? Reach out and see. See where it is that you find yourself drawn to, my friends.

Creating a daily practice is essential

This work of daily grounding, meditation and meeting the soul needs to be practiced daily or very regularly so that it becomes engrained in the human psyche. While it is your strong resolution that will bring forward this work, it must be practiced daily or on a very regular basis so that it is engrained and makes sense. Then it will become a practice that is reached for automatically, like a favorite coat or a pair of boots when it is raining. These will be the practices that you reach for when it is necessary for you to do so.

Grounding is the place to start. This must be done every day and is an important beginning place for the work that we do together. Once the grounding has been established, the next step in the practice is to connect deeply into yourself, into your soul. This is achieved by intention. We ask for the connection to soul, which is an ancient and wise place within, an energy that comes forward and takes its place within you. When you ground and set your intention to be in and with the soul, you will discover that there is a place within that is aligned with the Divine and with your highest interests. It is this place within that has been waiting to come forward, like a ship within you that will steady and bring forward the next steps for you.

Now everyone is on a different path in this respect; the soul is an individual and unique experience for each one of you. The soul is the pathway to one's own eternal being and it is a beautiful and light-filled place that brings harmony and an internal steadiness. In making a connection deep within your soul, you can ask for the soul to come forward, to be an integral and important part of your being.

This will give you a sense of continuity because the soul has been around for many millennia and it is a place of great depth, light, wisdom and steadiness. It is important for you to be able to access this place. It is not a mystery. It is not something that is a difficult place to reach. It simply requires intention, grounding and a deliberate connection to be made, so that the energies of the soul can be brought forward.

For many, this will be an easy and natural connection, but for others, it will require a little work to remember, connect and even perhaps to believe that there is a soul. Of course there is! Everybody has a soul and a soul purpose, and it is the reconnection with that soul's purpose and that soul's energy that will drive this next stage of re-alignment with the Divine. It is a powerful and indeed joyful place to be in touch with, this internal, eternal energy that drives us forward.

It is a place of great light, joy and peace. A real burden is lifted in the reconnection with this place of internal wisdom. Do not underestimate the power of this connection. It brings forth your Divine essence and your purpose in this world. It brings forth the remembrance of the Divine and the spiritual aspects of your being. It is therefore an important connection and one to be practiced every day.

Expanding your energy

I hope that you are enjoying the steps that we are taking. It does not need to be a difficult or onerous task that you undertake. It is not something that needs to cause you great pain or strain. What we are hoping to do is to bypass a lot of the processing that has been done in years gone by and to move into connection with others on a spiritual level.

This is done by raising your awareness and raising your vibration, which will bring to light and to the surface certain elements of your life's process and unresolved issues.

If you can see them in the context of simply being an energetic block that needs to move through you, you do not need to get stuck in the storyline of what is being expelled. The process is to let these bubbles of energy move through you and escape—not getting caught up in process or the story behind them, but simply letting things move through.

In the energetic expansion that you are practicing, there will be things that you bump up against and need some assistance with, but in the main, it is simply a case of expanding your energy outwards, into the larger realm. The energies at this time have accelerated, which means that when you reach these higher energies, you will find companionship. I think a lot of people will appreciate the new work that is being done, so that a new level of companionship can be acquired in the context of one's spiritual being and spiritual progression.

You may be asking: "What does that mean?" It means that there are a lot of souls and spirits dealing with this change and asking the same questions. A lot of the soul's work is to achieve a level of coherence and consistency with the expansion into the greater energetic field.

The practice of soul connection

Let us practice:

- *Start by grounding solidly into the Earth.*

- *Set an intention to be grounded and attuned to the Earth's energy.*

- *Focus into the soul's energy.*

- *Bring forth the soul's light by intention to connect with the soul.*

- *As you connect with the soul, expand the soul's light and energy out into the rest of the body.*

- *Expand the soul's light and energy out into the energy field.*

- *Expand the soul's light and energy out beyond the energy field and into the larger realm.*

- *Through your intention, connect with higher beings and with Divine energy.*

- *Through your connection with Divine energy, expand your energetic field.*

- *And stay here for a few minutes, feeling your essence, presence, peace and expansiveness.*

- *Then come back into the body, back to the ground and back to one's own self.*

- *And take time to integrate the experience, perhaps reflecting on your experience in writing.*

This important process forms the basis of a daily meditation or prayer practice. This daily practice is the essential cornerstone of this work. It is repeated in full in the soul practice summary on the last page of our teachings so that you can go quickly every day and begin your daily meditation/prayer practice. Record your thoughts and experiences in a notebook, journal or diary as you try this out and let it develop and see where this goes. It is a powerful practice.

Working with your spirit guide team

I will take you now on a journey where you will be working with your own spirit guide team.

- *Begin the grounding process.*

- *Bring yourself into alignment with your soul.*

- *Surround yourself in white light and ask for Divine protection and for any channelings to come from the highest energies and for your Divine good only.*

- *Call upon your spirit guides.*

You will find that your spirit guides come to you because it is exciting for them to be in touch with your human journey, which will have been a time of trial for you in some ways. They are here to support and help you on your journey. For many of you this is a time of joyful reunion because it is a remembrance of a past time when this connection was important to them and to you. It is the beginning of a new relationship from spirit to spirit in this current moment; it is a developing relationship where you become accustomed to speaking to and being with your spirit guide and giving them the opportunity to speak to you and perhaps to channel with them.

I am not going to teach you to channel because there are established schools which can teach you to channel with your spirit guide. I simply wish to open the door to the idea that you always have a spirit guide team around you, who can be called upon to be of assistance to you as you move through your life work and tasks. It may be difficult to remember this in the daily grind of life, but it is always possible, and it can be a joyful and illuminating experience for you.

Think about this and give it a go, and then of course if you are intrigued, you can reach out and find places to learn more.

Working with others

While it is difficult to work with others in coming into your spiritual self, this is important. It is important to be part of a group and to share the spiritual journey with others. It is essential to speak openly to others about the journey that you are on, and to find other similar-minded people and groups. This is a crucial aspect of this work—it is not simply about being alone. Reach out to others in the groups in which you congregate or socialize—to others in spiritual communities local to you. Seek out the spiritual accompaniment of others. They need not have matching views, as long as they have a spiritual component to their lives which is a central core value and of great interest to them.

This needs to be done carefully because you do not want to unfurl the flag and find it sagging without wind. There needs to be a wind to haul your sail aloft and give it room to breathe and to move your ship forward. So, it is important not to stay in groups where there is no wind, but to find the wind and to find others who can set sail with you. I'm sorry for using this analogy quite so strongly, but it is a good analogy: there is a journey, there is a fair wind that will take you on that journey and there are others who can share the journey with you. And so, in setting sail, it is important to find the group and collective that can help you move forward on your journey.

This work is simply not sustainable on your own. It is a collective endeavor now. It is not a case of going into the desert, or to a nunnery, or to a chamber to stay celibate and alone. It is now necessary to move outwards and forwards, to congregate with others and be part of something larger.

I would encourage you to ask yourself: "What is it that I need to explore in this context? What is it that I need to be aware of? What is it that I need to ask? Who can be my partners? Who can congregate with me in this way?"

I don't think it is hard to imagine that there is a new way of being, a new way of communicating and connecting with others. I think that is all imaginable and understandable, but the practice of it is another matter. Are there others that you can practice this with? Who in your friendship group and in your social environment would be open to a little bit of practice of these ideas?

You may be thinking: "What would be asked of them?" What would be necessary is simply a place to congregate, even a place where you can have coffee and enjoy each other's company, but it needs to be a place that is of high vibration. Whether it is a church or a place in nature, it is important that it has a good vibration.

Do not open to the spirit world where there is negative and dark energy. If you perceive this, do not stay; do not open yourselves to the possibility of a lower energy being present because that will simply misalign the information and cause havoc and possibly distress.

This work must be done with great dignity. Always clear the space. Always give yourself some time in prayer. Always seek to call in the most Divine energy to surround you and protect you, to clear any negative energy and to align you with the highest energies so that you are prepared and ready to receive only the most Divine energies that are in your best interests. Ask for the protection of the Divine. In that realm, there is a very strong protection for you as you open yourself to the possibility of connecting with others in light. If your intention is to connect to others in light, then that will be the outcome.

So, let us practice this by choosing a friend, relative, colleague or even an animal and asking for Divine light to surround you and protect you and then reaching out to that person and saying, "Can you hear me?"

Give it a go. See if you get a response. What does that person say back to you? You are of course connecting with their Higher Self, so they may not be attuned yet and may not consciously at this moment hear you, but they may think of you—there may be a bell ringing somewhere that might suggest to them that they should contact you.

Stepping into the unknown— mind the gap!

We are entering into a new segment of the work where I will guide you into a deeper place. This is a practice which is more valuable if it can become a consistent and regular practice. It will then become a habitual practice that will give you grounding and expansion so that you can connect to this new work and communicate with others in a more subtle fashion.

There is a gap that needs to be filled. You are leaping into the unknown in taking this next step. It is important that you are aware of the step that you are taking, and you consider and clarify the best way to progress. It is a step into the unknown, but you will have a sense of trust and expectation that the next step will emerge in its own time and place. You will have a trust that there will not be an emptiness, but rather a fullness that will come upon you: a presence and knowing, a sense of intuitive rightness that will grow within you while this work is being undertaken.

So how does this begin? Well, you have grounded. You have expanded. You might see that in the growth of expansion, you are in your heart. Have you given attention to your heart and to your soul's connection? From that place, the next step is to ask: "Where are we now?" "What's here now?" "What's arising within me that needs attention? What's here now for my next steps?"

You are asking your heart and your soul for this information. While you might not have an immediate, concrete and decisive answer, there may be a whisper. There may be a silence. There may be a consideration required. You are looking for a movement of the soul. You are looking for a whisper, a longing, a discernment. Here you can awaken to the next steps in your soul's commitment to you, your soul's life journey with you. Your next steps are not unknown in the soul's context, but now there is a movement forward in the discernment process: a knowing, a whispering, a guiding.

Can you trust that movement, guiding, whisper? What is being said? What is coming forward? How do the next steps appear to be forming? This can seem like a frightening or exciting time of anticipation: What will come next? How will this unfold? What is the next step?

It may not come forward immediately. That is why I am saying it is a practice. It is a discernment. It may take time. It may take some patience and anticipation of those next steps. Do you have your journal at hand? Do you have some quiet space for contemplation? Do you have a light, a candle? Keep asking the questions. Keep taking this journey. Keep being aware and awake to the next steps in your soul's journey with you.

It is a time of great excitement and anticipation.

Expanding on the practice

I would like to expand on what is meant by "grounding," what is meant by "expanding," and what is meant by "participation in the collective other." These aspects are important because they are the building blocks for a solid connection to yourself, to the spirit world and to others. I cannot emphasize enough how important these elements are in bringing together this work in a coherent and timely fashion.

The grounding process is the most important because in the times of change which are coming and are here now, it is much harder to ground than it has been in the past. There are increased levels of anxiety, and this is becoming more problematic for the grounding process. So, where in the past you have been able to focus on grounding through the energy levels and down into the core of the Earth, this is not working as well anymore because there is a blockage. There is a level of disconnection as the foundations of the known world are changing and shifting.

The grounding process is more important than ever and is one which will bring more consolidation to the work already done in your lifetime and in the lifetimes of all human beings who are participating in this process. It is an important step. While it may seem fundamental and easy to rush over, it is not to be abbreviated. I would like to say one more time that practicing the grounding process every day is essential, even when you are not thinking of meditating, praying or giving time to the work that we are doing together.

Grounding should be a fundamental step every day. At the beginning of every day, ground into the Earth and into the Earth's energy field. If possible, go into the garden or into a green space, take off your shoes and spend some time in bare feet grounding into the earth of the garden or park, bringing your energy field into balance.

It is an important part of your daily practice: it brings great energy to you, balances the energy field, brings down tension, reconnects the cells of the body to the spiritual realm, brings harmony and balance. It allows you to connect into the soul, and to connect with the heart. This is a strong and centered place that will bring health benefits if it is done daily.

So that is Step One. Step Two is expanding: aligning with the Divine, with the soul's purpose and energy and bringing this through and out into daily life. This brings you into connection with the heart center, with the core center, with the "nothing place" that is the center of all being. It is a very powerful and balanced place to connect with, to be aligned with, and to act from. To bring energy out from this place gives great wisdom and a sense of being at peace and on purpose.

This place is different for everyone. It is not possible for me to be more concrete and specific than this because for each one of you there is a very different place, a different stage, a different sense of priorities because your life purpose is unique. I encourage you to explore, to use the exercises I have given to connect with and expand the soul throughout the body, the energy field, and out into the spiritual realm and into contact with others.

It is an exciting place. It is not a vulnerable place. It is not a scary place. It is a very powerful and subtle place where you are in your own power, and you are accessible and amenable to all around you because you are at peace. So, it is a very important place and an important practice. Again, it is a daily practice that will bring many benefits as it becomes automatic and habitual.

Step Three is, from a grounded and soul place, to reach out and to see, what is around you, what is available to you? What is coming into your life, whether through others, through interactions with others or indeed through choices that you make from those interactions with others that you might not otherwise have thought of?

This is why it is important to be in contact with and fluent in the language of spiritual discernment and your own way forward because it is in interactions with other people that you begin to understand the larger dimensions of your life, and the larger community purpose of which you form a part. You have a part to play in the environment and the society in which you live, and this can only be discerned by an interaction with that society and environment. Then you will see where you fit in, what your purpose is, what your place is and how you can contribute.

It is not possible to do this work alone or in isolation. It must be done with others, whether through an online group, a local spiritual prayer group, church, or other organization with which you resonate. It does not even need to be discussed specifically and explicitly. Whatever you are doing together, the important thing is that you all have a joint interest in meditating or being in a spiritual dimension. That is sufficient for you to find a way to do this work in your own fashion. This is a blueprint, but it is not set in stone.

There are many ways to practice this material. There are many ways to accommodate existing spiritual norms. It is a simple practice that can be adapted to many types of spiritual and environmental groups. It cannot be done in isolation because it requires the input and participation of others.

Reaching out to the collective

The daily practice of this work is very important because it grounds and expands you into the next steps of the process. What you do now is the same spiritual endeavor that others have undertaken throughout the history of humankind. It is expanding out into the universe and being part of the whole.

While earlier humans had this capacity, it has been forgotten in the human socialization process because it has not been necessary in the social gatherings that you have in current times. Now you will find that it is once again important to reach out and gain more clarity from the spiritual realm, from your guides, from others and from the collective.

Many of you have become disconnected from the spiritual realm and have doubts about its existence. Many think that there is only the mind and the intellectual capacity, but this now needs to be broken down because reaching out beyond this is a necessity. It is an important part of the evolution of humanity. Reaching out into the spiritual realm in a way that is safe, connected and trusting will give you a better connection with yourself, your soul, your purpose and the way forward into the next steps of your development.

I am excited about this journey for you. It is one of grace, good humor, delight and excitement to rediscover a glorious place within you that can help you reach out to others and enable you to feel connected and part of something much bigger. That is so important now, and the simple exercises that we have shown you are the way to begin, first alone and then with a group. Reach out to connect with others, with family, with friends, with the outside world and see how this develops and how it becomes an imaginable and necessary part of your ordinary lives.

It is an evolution that is beyond the internet, smart-phone, television or the telephone. It is now time for direct communication through the medium of spirit. That is the excitement of this time and one to be cherished and practiced daily.

IV. INTEGRATION AND ILLUMINATION: LIVING THE WORK IN THE WORLD

Bringing this work into focus and connecting with others

I t is a time of great change. I do not wish to be a difficult and challenging mentor, but of course, there is work always to be done to bring this work into focus for each one of you. The focus is your own evolution—it is the connection with the Earth, with your soul, and with the other that is important.

You are very much the foundation of the work that we do together because you have the skills, the participation and the intention to bring this work through. There is nothing to fear about this work. It has been done for many millennia by many peoples, indeed throughout the universe, and it is not a unique process. It is a simple process that has brought center-ing, grounding, connection and communication throughout the universe.

We are all light beings, and we all have this opportu-nity now to connect, to communicate and to discuss with you directly how you can evolve and how you can live better and more connected lives. You see how the disconnection in the world is causing such enormous suffering. It is not connection through the medium of telephone, social media or television that is important. It is something that is far greater, more organic and complete. It is the connection between two people, between two galaxies even, that is resonant through the light beings that you are.

It is not an easy concept, perhaps, but it is a concept that brings with it the need for a practice, faith and trust that this is the truth and there is something to gain from your practice of this work now. I would like you to focus on a new way forward, a new way to be in the world, which is not an intellectual or heady way of being, but something based in the body's energetic field: a heart and soul approach to how connection and communication can be established between individuals and peoples throughout the world.

It is a fabulous opportunity to connect and communicate with others and this can best be done in a group where it is possible to say to the other: "Well, what do you think we talked about? What do you think we said? What do you think we are communicating together?" It will be interesting for you to understand how that operates, how and when you are connecting and when you are not. This is the group work that needs to take place and needs to be practiced.

So how to begin? I think with your own questions, your own intuitions, your own life force that comes through with your soul's connection into the realm that says: *"Well, what now? I am afraid of this space. This lack of connection, this venturing into the void. I am afraid of this. I am not sure what is happening. I am not sure what we are doing. I feel afraid. I don't feel any connection. I don't understand why we are doing this. I'm not enjoying this at all. I'm not sure what this is about. I'm very afraid. I don't think I want to do this anymore. I'm coming through this suddenly. Yes, I can stop. But I don't want to. I can just let this empty space be there. Something is moving.*

Something is there. There is a warmth. A subtle presence. Fear—I'm not sure what that is. I'm just going stay with it. It takes time. Getting stronger. Inkling of joy. Inkling of presence. Something is here. Lots of energy. Lots of heat and light. I don't know where this is going, though. I'm afraid. I'm not sure what I'm doing here. I'm getting a bit concerned again. Strong energy. Just letting go, letting go. That's what this is about. Letting go. Oh, just let it go. Feeling it in the back of my neck. My spine. I'm letting things go. Oh, yes, letting it go. Not taking in the story—just letting it go. Really just letting it go."

Communicating directly

Practice this process every day. I'm not going to give you more than this because you already know the core work that needs to be done, and it is simply a practice.

Keep a journal. Keep track of the experiences that you are having. Reach out and connect with others and see what is happening for them, what they tell you, what they say to you. It may be that their higher selves are talking to you, in a communication straight from the heart and soul of the person you are connecting with.

Try this also with your animals and with people who you know quite well because you will be able to see how they resonate with you. They may say something that you would expect them to say. Perhaps sometimes they will share something unexpected, something more direct and forthright than you are used to hearing from them, but they will have something to say to you which is valuable.

It might not always be the best thing to come straight to them and say: "are you thinking this?" They may not know themselves that this is where they are at, but you can elicit this information by gentle indirect questioning that might not upset or frighten the person that you are speaking to.

So here we are at a new beginning, a new type of work, a new place that can be of benefit to humanity. I would like you to embed this practice, to begin to evolve the communication process and the evolution process by connecting to others by direct communication. Practice and discuss in your groups and see where this material goes.

As you do this, it will bring this practice into focus for you so that you can move forward with a sense of a whole: that this is a whole body of work which will allow you to connect into something bigger in times that may be disruptive, difficult and frightening. You have this roadmap. You have this way forward. You have this way of connecting with others in a way that does not require communication by telephone, by social media or by other types of connection that may or may not be available to you at that moment. This connection is always available, and the spirit world is always here to support you.

Principles of this work and practice

This work can be encapsulated in two simple principles.

The first principle is that it is important to ground and to be fully present on the Earth, not to be half present, not to be somewhere else, not to be thinking of other things, but to be fully present in the moment and to work most solidly on being grounded, present, open and receptive. This is a first and basic tenet of the work that is to be done.

The second principle is that there is a new way of being. There is a new evolution of the spirit that requires you to bring your soul forward, to deepen your connection into your soul and to move outwards. Your soul is a very high vibrational being and therefore brings with it safety from lower astral beings. When you are connected to your soul, these low-density beings will not affect you.

Your life will inevitably change in the coming years, and I would like to emphasize that this is a practice for millennia. It is a practice that will stand you in good stead for these changes. Please work daily to bring this practice into focus and into alignment with your changing life. This is what I desire for you. It is a lifeline, and it is a helpful tool to have in your toolbox, so that you can be at one with your neighbors and yet in your own space.

There is a lot of energy and change around now and it is with great sympathy that we say that with difficult world events emerging, it is important to begin these grounding exercises as soon as possible and to develop this practice quickly. It is the way that you will find your own equilibrium and connect with others by being more cognizant of the way forward.

The grounding exercises are simple for a reason. Where they will be required in times of stress, your practice is your centering, grounding alignment process. It is an alignment process that will bring you into balance by not being caught up in the news of the day which spreads a sense of urgency and panic. It is important not to connect with this negative energy. Every time you feel this happening, dig deep and give yourself the time and space to do this practice.

Start now and be of good cheer. Do not connect into the negativity around you. This work is part of a process to begin to raise your vibration and connect with others in a more positive state. Reach out to others and form a group to bring through the connection that you are practicing. Work diligently with this material, then bring it through into a group setting, which can be anything from a meditation group to a church group to a meeting with others of like mindedness who wish to participate in this type of work and are drawn to say: "let's work together."

While you are practicing diligently, it is easy to forget that this message also needs to go out to many people and it is in your connection with the larger whole that you will bring forward this material carefully and diligently. So, you are saying, "Friends and colleagues, here is a way forward. Here is my understanding of the beginnings of a new life, and we will help each other to perceive and receive these messages from our guides, from the larger whole, and from the Divine." And it is from the Divine that these messages come.

We are all working together on this material. You are not alone. We are all connected into one larger whole. There is no separation. We are all one and we stretch our souls' remembering by meeting together, reaching out and being with others who are also reaching out. This is an important step and can be achieved in many ways. It is not necessary to say that this is exactly what we are doing, but the intention is to reach out and to be part of the larger whole, to bring this work through to others and to receive and perceive the aspect of being part of this larger gathering.

Do not be afraid of not knowing, and of the void. Do not be afraid of the attitude of others who do not understand or do not want you to participate in this work.

V. THE FULFILLMENT OF THE JOURNEY: BECOMING A LIGHT FOR AND WITH OTHERS

How this will help you

This process will help you in the coming years. It will help your soul to solidify and progress toward the evolution you hope to achieve in this lifetime. Practice this material with as much integrity as you can. It is not a simple task as there is a lifetime of objections or limitations in processing the work we do together. Nevertheless, it helps you to do this work and to enter a new way of living that will give you such great joy and benefit in connecting with others directly.

This is where humanity is heading now. There is no need for barriers because at this level, everyone desires connection and communication. Everyone is here for that purpose. It is not an accident that are reading this material. You will have your own way of processing your life's work, but also, there is a need and desire that you and everyone else shares currently: to communicate more directly. This can be done with practice.

We are not separate. We are all part of the same wholeness and oneness that is the reality of spirit. So do not be afraid of this work. Do not think that this does not apply in your circumstance or situation because it is a great benefit to be able to communicate in this way and will hold you in good stead for your future life.

While there will be more material to share with you in the future, including group practice, the essential component of this material is the practice I have outlined and repeat in the section to follow. You can simply go to the last page of these teachings and begin the practice daily. Record your thoughts and experiences in a notebook, journal or diary as you try this out. Let it develop and see where this goes.

It is a powerful practice which will give you a good grounding and level of experience that will help to build a container for you to bring more of this work forward in due course.

Some practical tips from Laura

The process of soul connection need not take long—15 or 20 minutes is enough, I find, depending on how long it takes to clear my mind and focus on the steps.

If you are not used to praying or meditating regularly, and are not sure how to start, a few tips may help you:

- *Make sure you have time;*
- *Find a quiet place where you will not be disturbed;*
- *Make yourself comfortable;*
- *Light a candle;*
- *Start with some deep breathing into your belly;*
- *Consciously let go of your day and your to-do list;*
- *Once you feel a little space in your mind, try to follow the steps in the Soul Practice that follows.*

VI. THE SOUL PRACTICE: A DAILY SEQUENCE FOR GROUNDING AND CONNECTION

- *Find a quiet place to sit where you will not be disturbed.*

- *Start by grounding solidly into the Earth with your intention. Just draw a line from your body down into the center of the Earth and make contact with the Earth's energy.*

- *Set an intention to be grounded and attuned to the Earth's energy.*

- *Focus into your soul's energy, which is in and around your body.*

- *Bring forth your soul's light by intention to connect with the soul. Just intend to connect with your soul, and you will. It may take a while to feel it.*

- *As you connect with the soul, expand your soul's light and energy out into the rest of your body.*

- *Expand your soul's light and energy out beyond your body and into your energy field, which surrounds your body.*

- *Expand your soul's light and energy out beyond your own energy field and into the larger realm.*

- *Through your intention, connect with higher beings and with Divine energy.*

- *Through your connection with Divine energy, expand your own energetic field which expands beyond your physical body.*

- *And stay here for a few minutes, feeling your own essence, presence, peace and expansiveness.*

- *Then come back into your body, back to the ground and back to your own self.*

- *Take time to integrate the experience, perhaps in writing, and to investigate additional materials from Andraus and the Light Collective to support your practice, available at Spiritwoven.com.*

AFTERWORD

From KUAN YIN

Dear holders of the flame of the future,
If you are ready now to put down this book, to let go of these words on a page, then there is one last thing that we would ask you to do.

We would ask you to just sit for a moment. And as you sit just take a few deep breaths. These deep breaths are always a way in, into your being.

As you take these few deep breaths, intend to let what is important for you to know be absorbed into your knowing, absorbed into your heart, resonating with the essence of you. Hold those energies within and throughout the whole of you.

Perhaps nothing on the surface changes. Perhaps there is a shift in language. Perhaps there is a shift in how you are seeing some small part of the Earth's creation or the gift of your own physical being. And perhaps there is only a shift in how you hear the news of the day and what you are able to hold, in an expanded sense of knowing.

Trust that what is important for you has been received. And it has been received with gratitude by the essence of your being, which seeks always to have that greater sense of your being, that connection to greater knowing, expanded consciousness, and a more open heart reinforced, nourished, supported.

Just as when you eat, you are not fully aware of how what you have taken in is used by the entirety of your body, so you cannot know how the energies and the ideas that you have encountered here are becoming integrated into the wholeness of your being. But know that it is so.

Let yourself dream of what is to be. And let yourself know that you are a part of the becoming of all that will be.

✴

ACKNOWLEDGMENTS

would not be in deep relationship with Spirit and able to bring forward this book without all the love and support that has allowed me to open to living a full life in earthly and spiritual terms. My family gave me a strong foundation of love and freedom.

At different points in my life and in very different ways Bob Sinclair, Carol Drexler, Joan Sweeney, Katherine Gable, Elizabeth Foley, Diana Meunz Chen and Uri Herscher have all been a part of helping me find my way home.

My beloved wife of 28 years, Susan Vogelfang, designer of my beautiful website and the cover art for this book, offers her love and support always.

Certainly, finding my way with this book has been greatly aided by my editor Jennifer Browdy.

I am truly grateful for Laura Craig's friendship and beautiful channeling, which are woven into the whole of this work.

ABOUT THE AUTHOR

Kathryn Girard, Ed.D., has served as a channel for Kuan Yin and other guides since 1987. Retirement from a successful career as an educational and arts executive in 2020 enabled her to partner more fully with a team of spirit guides who are urgently focused on supporting the expansion of Light for individuals, humanity and the planet. A skilled textile weaver, Kathryn considers herself a weaver of cloth, hearts, words, and ideas. For information on coaching, workshops and classes, as well as related teachings, worksheets, meditations and audio recordings, visit Kathryn's website: Spiritwoven.com.

www.ingramcontent.com/pod-product-compliance
Lightning Source LLC
Chambersburg PA
CBHW032229050726
47591CB00001B/324